Race, Culture and Mental Illness in the International Criminal Court's Ongwen Judgment: Biases and Blindspots

Beth S. Lyons

Race, Culture and Mental Illness in the International Criminal Court's Ongwen Judgment: Biases and Blindspots

palgrave
macmillan

Beth S. Lyons
New Jersey, USA

ISBN 978-3-031-73682-7 ISBN 978-3-031-73683-4 (eBook)
https://doi.org/10.1007/978-3-031-73683-4

This Palgrave Macmillan imprint is published by the registered company Springer Nature Switzerland AG.
The registered company address is: Gewerbestrasse 11, 6330 Cham, Switzerland

Background to the *Ongwen* Case

Dominic Ongwen was abducted on his way to school in 1987 by the Lord's Resistance Army ("LRA") in Northern Uganda, when he was eight or nine years old and trafficked as a child soldier. Over a period of 27 years in the LRA, Mr. Ongwen made numerous failed attempts to escape, and was punished and imprisoned in the LRA for these attempts. Mr. Ongwen finally succeeded in escaping in late December 2014. In January 2015, Mr. Ongwen surrendered to the International Criminal Court ("ICC") in the Central African Republic on the ICC's arrest warrant[1] and was transferred to The Hague.

Mr. Ongwen, a mentally ill and mentally disabled defendant, was prosecuted on an ICC indictment of 70 charges, including war crimes and crimes against humanity and multiple forms of liability. The charges included sexual and gender based crimes and conscripting child soldiers (like himself).[2] Mr. Ongwen's defence, under the ICC's Rome Statute, Article 31(1)(a) and (d), was that he was not responsible for the crimes of

[1] The original ICC arrest warrant (8 July 2005) was issued for Joseph Kony, Vincent Otti, Raska Lukwiya, Okot Odhiambo and Dominic Ongwen. *See*, ICC - Uganda (archive.ph). Only Kony and Ongwen are still alive. The Prosecution stipulated during trial that Vincent Otti was killed on the order of Joseph Kony.

[2] *Prosecutor v. Ongwen*, ICC-02/04-01/15-422-Red, Decision on the confirmation of charges against Dominic Ongwen (March 23, 2016), CR2016_02331.PDF (icc-cpi.int) ("COC Decision" or "indictment").

the LRA, based on his mental illnesses and duress, stemming from his abduction and subsequent coercion and indoctrination under Joseph Kony within the LRA. In February 2021, Trial Chamber IX convicted Dominic Ongwen of 61 charges and two modes of liability. In May 2021, he was sentenced to 25 years' incarceration. The Appeals Chamber affirmed the Trial Judgment's convictions and sentence on 15 December 2022.

The *Ongwen* case is the most complex single defendant case to date at the ICC. The links listed below may be helpful to the reader.[3] The relevant pleadings of all Parties—Prosecution, Defence and Victims' Representatives—are cited within these documents. Additional references and links are found in Chaps. 1 and 2.

[3] ICC Case Information Sheet provides an abbreviated procedural history at Case Information Sheet (icc-cpi.int). a) Summary of Trial Judgment, Ongwen case: summary of the verdict, 4 February 2021 (icc-cpi.int); b) Trial Judgment ("TJ"), 4 February 2021 at CR2021_01026.PDF (icc-cpi.int); c) Summary of Sentence, Summary of the delivery of the sentence on 6 May 2021 (icc-cpi.int); d) Trial Judgment on Sentence, 6 May 2021 at CR2021_04230.PDF (icc-cpi.int); e) Summary of Appeal Judgment, 2022-12-15-ongwen-judgment-summary-eng.pdf (icc-cpi.int); f) Appeal Judgment on Defence Appeal Against Convictions ("AJ"), 15 December 2022 at CR2022_07146.PDF (icc-cpi.int); g) Appeal Judgment on Sentence, 15 December 2022 at CR2022_07148.PDF (icc-cpi.int)

Acknowledgments

I want to thank my colleagues and friends, who are named in each chapter, for reading (and, sometimes, re-reading) previous drafts of the chapters which became this book. Both they and the anonymous reviewers have provided invaluable assistance and generously contributed their expertise and time. I am grateful to those individuals whom I have never met, but responded positively to my e-mail requests for help. I would also like to thank the *Ongwen* Defence team members, including our interns and volunteer lawyers, with whom I have worked over the years. Defence work is a team undertaking.

I would like to especially acknowledge five other individuals who made this book possible: Professor Lennox S. Hinds, whose ideological leadership and clarity have inspired and guided me over decades, including through the "law and politics" conundrum and who recommended me for my first case at the ICTR 20 years ago; Chief Charles A. Taku, with whom I have worked on international criminal cases at the ICTR and ICC for almost two decades, and whose ideological guidance and legal support have sustained me, particularly throughout the *Ongwen* case; Professor Emilio Ovuga and Dr. Dickens Akena, whose expertise provided the "backbone" of the *Ongwen* Defence and who patiently educated me and the Defence team about mental illness; and Mr. Dominic Ongwen, who accepted me as a co-counsel and trusted me to represent him, and without whom there would be no *Ongwen* case to write about and this book would not exist.

Author's Note

I would like to share a few points about the writing of this book. First, I have been a Defence counsel in the *Ongwen* case since 2017 and I am an advocate of the *Ongwen* Defence. I have litigated the affirmative defence of mental disease or defect under the Rome Statute, Article 31(1)(a) at trial and on appeal. Hence, I make no pretenses of neutrality, objectivity or being unbiased. As a trial lawyer, I have tried to curb my "knee-jerk" response to re-litigate the case in this book. Of course, some of the Defence arguments made during the trial are repeated here, and I invite readers to look at the original documents cited in the footnotes. The Trial Chamber decisions and Judgment summarize the positions of all the Parties in the case, with links to pleadings.

Second, converting litigation arguments into themes or conclusions for this book has been a formidable task. Arguments cannot simply be cut and pasted into a different format. While there is a dialectical relationship between theory and practice, the process of extracting theory out of practice is not spontaneous or "self-explanatory." It is often difficult to formulate the broader implications of one's practice, especially in a complex case with a myriad of legal issues of first impression, such as in *Ongwen.*

Third, the analytical framework of this book, using the concept of judicial biases and blindspots, may be criticized by some readers as an "ableist" construct because of the term "blindspot." I accept that language is political, and that usage of certain terms can be discriminatory and can enforce inequality. On its own, the word "blindspot" is pejorative, offensive and discriminatory to persons who are visually impaired, or have no sight at all; it implicitly assumes that to be sighted is a superior state.

But an analysis of language must consider the context and intent to determine whether a word is ableist, or—for that matter—any "-ist" such as racist, sexist, ageist, homophobist, etc. It is the specific usage of the word—the "who, where, for what purpose and why"—which provides guidance as to its characterization.

Throughout the book, I use the word "blindspot" for its literal meaning, to refer to something that results in the inability to see, and which obstructs vision. I have added to the definition the inability to see or perceive a key component of a situation, to the detriment of the person who is viewing it. I have also linked the concepts of blindspot and bias which are in a symbiotic relationship: the blindspot is produced by biases, which feed and support its existence, while, in return, the blindspot ensures that the biases remain immutable, reinforcing the blindspot. This is discussed more in Chap. 1.

* * *

This book examines how race and culture operate in the *Ongwen* Trial Judgment, particularly the effects of judicial biases and blindspots on the Judgment's jurisprudence.[1] The impact of race and culture on the ICC has been studied, researched and criticized by persons with different expertise than I.[2] But less scrutiny has been given to how these factors shape the ICC's jurisprudence in the cases it adjudicates. Similarly, there is no dearth of printed and on-line materials available about the *Ongwen* case. But very few, if any, to my knowledge, have closely examined how race and culture "play out" in the courtroom, and their impact on the Court's jurisprudence.

---

[1] I focus on the *Ongwen* Trial Judgment in my analysis and examples, although my conclusions would also apply to the Appeal Judgment, which affirmed the Trial Judgment.

[2] *See* references in footnotes in Chaps. 1 and 2.

Chapter 1 discusses how biases and blindspots operate, and examines the racial and cultural judicial biases and blindspots and their impact on Mr. Ongwen's affirmative defences of mental disease or defect and duress (Rome Statute, Article 31(1)(a) and (d)), as well as on Mr. Ongwen's sentencing. I argue that the *Ongwen* Judges suffered from blindspots, based on racial and cultural biases, which prevented them from assessing the evidence in an impartial manner and correctly applying the law; and that these biases and blindspots were a significant factor in the Trial Chamber's rejection of Mr. Ongwen's affirmative defences of mental disease or defect and duress.

This resulted in the Trial Chamber's legal conclusions being flawed and defective, because the Chamber did not consider the impact of racial and cultural factors on its conclusions. The concept of blindspot, based on bias, connotes that the Judges simply were unable—on their own—to perceive or see these factors due to biases and blindspots. But it is also true that when the Chamber was made aware of racial and cultural factors by the Defence, in respect to mental illness and to the important role of spiritualism in duress, the Chamber made a conscious, voluntary choice *not* to consider these factors—either in its Judgment or for sentencing purposes. Thus, the Chamber not only could not, but also would not, consider racial and cultural factors.

Chapter 2 applies the concepts of bias and blindspot to mental disability. It discusses the Trial Chamber's failure to reasonably accommodate Mr. Ongwen's mental disability. Reasonable accommodation of disability concerns equal access to justice, and, its legal standard, as proposed in this chapter, should be a *prima facie* showing of disability. This standard is much lower than the legal standard for a finding of guilt, which is proof beyond a reasonable doubt, under the Rome Statute, Article 66. Mr. Ongwen, however, is both mentally ill and mentally disabled, and a different standard applies to the judicial determinations of each: exclusion of criminal responsibility based on mental disease or defect (burden of proof on Prosecution to disprove beyond a reasonable doubt) and reasonable accommodation for a mental disability (*prima facie* showing of disability). The *Ongwen* Judges, however, conflated the two standards, which resulted in violation of Mr. Ongwen's fair trial rights under the Rome Statute, Article 67. I propose, based on the

Ongwen case, that the ICC make available to defendants a presumption of mental disability, which could be invoked by the defendant, but only if s/he chooses to do so.

The "Ongwen Exception"

The essence of the *Ongwen* Trial Chamber's position on race and culture is best encapsulated in its judicially created "Ongwen Exception"[3] (discussed in Chap. 1) which threads through the Trial Judgment, and is even more salient in the recent *Ongwen* Reparations Order.[4] The term "Ongwen Exception" is not explicitly articulated in the Judgment, but this concept is based on the Trial Chamber's premise that the toxicity, manipulation of spiritualism and its rituals, and the unfathomable violence of the LRA affected vulnerable child abductees, but did not affect Mr. Ongwen.[5] Although he suffered the same harms as other victims of the LRA, including being forced to participate in the heinous killings of his fellow abductees, the Chamber does not "see" Mr. Ongwen as a victim of the LRA. It does not "see" his humanity and his culture. To the Chamber, Mr. Ongwen—the person—is another Black defendant in the dock at the ICC, who is invisible.

This racism inherent in the "Ongwen Exception" prompts the recurring, fundamental question: is it "just" judicial biases and blindspots or is it legal racism and culturism which are reflected in the *Ongwen* Judgment? In the book's Conclusions, I endeavor to define these terms and begin to explore this question. It is important because the legitimacy of the ICC and, more generally, of international justice is at stake. But, most significantly, the struggles of people to hold government and military leaderships accountable and to end their impunity for international crimes and violations of human rights, and to achieve justice for victims are being

---

[3] Lyons, Beth S., 13 April 2024, The Ongwen Chamber's Reparations Order and the "Ongwen Exception": A Concept of Dehumanization, Invisibility and Racism - Opinio Juris. In his Introduction, Chief Taku writes about "*Ongwen Exceptionalism*," which is an amalgamation of the Trial Chamber's racial and cultural biases and blindspots. I use the term "Ongwen Exception" in the book to convey the same concept.

[4] *Ongwen* Reparations Order, 28 February 2024, 0902ebd18078e195.pdf (icc-cpi.int).

[5] Trial Judgment ("TJ"): 906–930.

fought every day. If international justice, and particularly the ICC, is going to fulfil its legal function, then it must apply the rule of law equally to everyone. But, to date, the ICC has failed abysmally in this task.

The work of many people, cited in the footnotes, has contributed to my analysis in this book. I, however, am responsible for any errors.

Contents

About the Author

Beth S. Lyons is an international criminal defence and human rights lawyer. She is a co-counsel for Mr. Dominic Ongwen at the International Criminal Court, and previously represented Mr. Narcisse Arido in the *Bemba* et al. "Article 70" case at the ICC. She has represented clients at the ICTR, including Major François-Xavier Nzuwonemeye ("Military II" case), for whom she and Lead Counsel Chief Charles A. Taku (with the Defence team) won an acquittal on appeal in 2014. Although acquitted, Major Nzuwonemeye is still not free: since 2014, he has been illegally detained, first in a "safe house" in Arusha, Tanzania and now in a "safe house" in Niamey, Republic of Niger. In 2024, he has completed the 20-year sentence which was originally imposed on him by the ICTR Trial Chamber, plus four additional years, for crimes for which he was acquitted.

Beth is a former legal aid attorney in New York City. Since 1997, she has served as an Alternate Representative to the UN in New York for the International Association of Democratic Lawyers (IADL), a non-governmental organization in consultative II status with ECOSOC, and represented at UNICEF and UNESCO. She is a co-author, with Chief Charles A. Taku, of *In the Trenches: The Politicisation of International Justice at the International Criminal Tribunal for Rwanda* (Africa World Press, forthcoming).

Abbreviations

ADA	*Americans with Disabilities Act*
AFRC	*Armed Forces Revolutionary Council*
AFR. J. PSYCHIATRY	*African Journal of Psychiatry*
AJ	*Ongwen Appeal Judgment*
AJIL	*American Journal of International Law*
AM. UNIV. INT. LAW REV.	*American University International Law Review*
APA	*American Psychiatric Association*
AViDI-18	*Akena Visual Depression Inventory*
BR. J. PSYCHIATRY	*British Journal of Psychiatry*
CDF	*Civil Defence Forces*
CES-D	*Center for Epidemiologic Studies Depression Scale*
CIA	*Central Intelligence Agency*
COC	*Confirmation of Charges*
COLUM. HUM. RTS. L. REV.	*Columbia Human Rights Law Review*
CRPD	*Convention on the Rights of Persons with Disabilities*
CULT. MED. PSYCHIATRY	*Culture, Medicine and Psychiatry*

CURR. DIR. PSYCHOL. SCI.	*Current Directions in Psychological Science*
CV	*Curriculum vitae*
DA	*Dr. Dickens Akena*
DAJ	*Ongwen Defence Appeal Brief Against the Convictions in the Judgment*
DAS	*Ongwen Defence Appeal Against Sentence*
DBS	*Ongwen Defence Brief on Sentence*
DCB	*Ongwen Defence Closing Brief*
DSM-IV	*Diagnostic and Statistical Manual of Mental Disorders, Fourth Edition*
DSM-5	*Diagnostic and Statistical Manual of Mental Disorders, Fifth Edition*
EO	*Professor Emilio Ovuga*
FRONT. PSYCHIATRY	*Frontiers in Psychiatry*
GM	*Dr. Gillian Mezey*
GROJIL	*Groningen Journal of International Law*
IAT	*Implicit Association Test*
ICC	*International Criminal Court*
ICCPR	*International Covenant on Civil and Political Rights*
ICD	*International Classification of Diseases*
ICESCR	*International Covenant on Economic, Social and Cultural Rights*
ICTR	*International Criminal Tribunal for Rwanda*
ICTY	*International Criminal Tribunal for the former Yugoslavia*
IDP	*Internally displaced persons*
INT. CRIM. LAW REV.	*International Criminal Law Review*

INT. J. ENVIR. RES. PUBLIC. HEALTH	*International Journal of Environmental Research and Public Health*
J. APPL. RES. MEM. COGN.	*Journal of Applied Research in Memory and Cognition*
J. CLIN. EXP. NEUROPSYCHOL.	*Journal of Clinical and Experimental Neuropsychology*
J. FORENSIC SCI.	*Journal of Forensic Sciences*
J. INT. CRIM. JUSTICE	*Journal of International Criminal Justice*
J. NATL. MED. ASSOC.	*Journal of the National Medical Association*
JUST. SEC.	*Just Security*
LOND. REV. INT. LAW	*London Review of International Law*
LRA	*Lord's Resistance Army*
MDD	*Major Depressive Disorder*
MED. J. AUST.	*Medical Journal of Australia*
MENTAL HEALTH L. & POL'Y	*Mental Health Law and Policy*
M–FAST	*Miller Forensic Assessment of Symptoms Test*
MLC	*Movement for the Liberation of the Congo*
NEUROPSYCHOL. REV.	*Neuropsychology Review*
NOTRE DAME L. REV.	*Notre Dame Law Review*
NRA	*National Resistance Army*
OTP	*Office of the Prosecutor*
POE	*Panel of Experts*
PTSD	*Post-traumatic stress disorder*
RPA	*Rwandan Patriotic Army*
RPE	*ICC Rules of Procedure and Evidence*
RPF	*Rwandan Patriotic Front*
SCSL	*Special Court for Sierra Leone*
SENTENCE JUDGMENT	*Ongwen Trial Judgment on Sentence*
T	*Transcript*
TJ	*Ongwen Trial Judgment*

TRANSCULT. PSYCHIATRY	*Transcultural Psychiatry*
TOMM	*Test of Memory Malingering*
UDHR	*Universal Declaration of Human Rights*
UNGA	*UN General Assembly*
UPDF	*Uganda Peoples' Defence Forces*
W-P	*Prof. Roland Weierstall-Pust*

Introduction

By Chief Charles A. Taku,[1] Lead Counsel for Dominic Ongwen

This book is about racial and cultural judicial biases in the trial and conviction of Dominic Ongwen, a mentally disabled and mentally incapacitated child soldier, by the ICC for crimes in which he was a victim. The author characterizes the biases as blindspots. The author does not accuse the Judges of a deliberate policy of racial and cultural judicial biases or *animus*. Nevertheless, the institutional and personal lenses through which they visualized the accused, Dominic Ongwen, assessed the evidence and applied the law was tainted by racial and cultural judicial biases.

Chapter 1 of the book is a critical examination, from the author's perspective, of the assessment of the evidence which was adduced during trial, and the application of the law by the ICC's Trial Chamber IX to

[1] Chief Charles A. Taku, a Lead Counsel at the ICC, is a former Lead Counsel at the Special Court for Sierra Leone (SCSL) and the International Criminal Tribunal for Rwanda (ICTR). He is a former President of the International Criminal Court Bar Association (ICCBA), and has published widely, including on the ICC and Africa, international criminal law and the return of stolen cultural artifacts to the African Continent. He is based in the Netherlands and in the US. E-mail is charto_us@yahoo.com.

Dominic Ongwen's affirmative defences of mental disease or defect and duress, pursuant to Article 31(1)(a) and (d) of the Rome Statute. The author explains and demonstrates that the Chamber's rejection of the affirmative defences was tainted by racial and cultural judicial biases which she characterizes as blindspots.

In Chap. 2, the author examines the mental health disability of Mr. Ongwen and the deliberate failure by the Chamber to afford him reasonable accommodation during trial. The author examines the impact of bias and blindspots on his mental disability which violated his right of access to justice.

The evidence of Mr. Ongwen's mental disability was provided by Defence Experts, Professor Emilio Ovuga and Dr. Dickens Akena; by the Court-appointed Expert, Professor Joop de Jong; and by the ICC Detention Centre physicians. His treatment regime was provided to the Trial Chamber, with recommendations for reasonable accommodation due to his mental health disability. The Chamber prioritized proceeding with the trial over reasonable accommodations of the mental disability concerns of Mr. Ongwen, in violation of his right of access to justice, which he repeatedly asserted without success. The Chamber rejected his Rule 135[2] evaluation applications which are applicable to an accused person with current symptoms of mental illness, and did not take further action for him to be evaluated every 120 days or less.[3] The Chamber rejected the Defence requests for the evaluation of the mental condition of Mr. Ongwen, and in the Trial Judgment, rejected his affirmative defences. A professional article co-authored by Defence Expert Professor Emilio Ovuga and Prosecution Expert Dr. Catherine Abbo on *Orongo* and *Cen* possessions in a cultural context in Northern Uganda was submitted into evidence.[4] Further evidence on *cen* possessions was provided by an Acholi traditional healer, an *Ajwaka*.[5] This evidence provided distinctive features of *cen* and Acholi cultural-specific characteristics of

[2] Rule 135, ICC Rules of Procedure and Evidence (Medical examination of the accused)

[3] Rule 135 (4), ICC RPE.

[4] Emilio Ovuga and Catherine Abbo, *"Orongo" and "Cen" Spirit Possessions: Post-Traumatic Stress Disorder in a Cultural Context – Local Problem, Universal Disorder with Local Solutions in Northern Uganda,* in Martin, C., Preedy, V. and Patel, V. (eds), COMPREHENSIVE GUIDE TO POST-TRAUMATIC STRESS DISORDERS, Springer, Cham (2015), https://doi.org/10.1007/978-3-319-08359-9_89, filed as UGA-D26-0015-0197.

[5] T-183, 5 October 2018.

therapy within the Acholi cultural system. The Chamber did not rely on this evidence and Acholi cultural factors and mechanisms in its Trial Judgment and Sentencing Decision. However, in its Reparations Order at the end of the case, the Chamber decided, without a scientific evaluation of victims and witnesses or a scientifically validated study of *cen* and its distinctive features within the Acholi cultural system, that the manifestation of *cen* and traumatic symptoms in victims and some witnesses equated to what "western medicine would call mental illness."[6] The is a negation of the distinctive identity of cultural factors and the cultural mechanisms on which a majority of victims of the conflict in Northern Uganda have relied for healing and rebuilding their lives and their communities. This is tantamount to racial and cultural bias against Mr. Ongwen and the Acholi cultural system.

The record of racial and cultural judicial biases is discernible from the opening statement at trial of the ICC Chief Prosecutor Fatou Bensouda on 6 December 2016 and the complaints which were made by Mr. Ongwen. The Chief Prosecutor submitted that "People following the case against Dominic Ongwen may do so with mixed emotions" [because] "he must have gone through the trauma of separation from his family, brutalisation by his captors, and initiation into the violence of the LRA way of life," [and that] "the evidence of many child victims in this case, in other circumstances, may be the story of the accused himself."[7]

The denial by the Trial Chamber of reasonable accommodation during trial, the rejection of affirmative defences and rejection, without sufficient reasoning, of substantially diminished mental capacity during sentencing due to his mental illness, form the basis for the characterization of the catalogue of racial and cultural biases as *"The Ongwen Exceptionalism."* This *Ongwen Exceptionalism* meant that everyone who was exposed to the criminal environment of the LRA and suffered the violations which the

---

[6] Reparations Order, 28 February 2024, para. 240: "The Chamber notes that some of the witnesses and victims referred to 'spiritual disturbances' or claimed to have experienced the phenomena referred to throughout the proceedings as '*cen*'… the Chamber considered the evidence that '*cen*' represents the vengeful spirits of those who have died a violent death, and are commonly used to interpret what western medicine would call 'mental illness.'"

[7] T-26, p. 36, ll. 1–9.

Chief Prosecutor submitted Mr. Ongwen suffered, suffered from mental sickness—but not Mr. Ongwen.

This was demonstrated by the total rejection of the long-lasting mental health consequences of child soldiering on Mr. Ongwen, based on the fact that the harms of child soldiering are not extinguished by chronological age for the purpose of criminal responsibility pursuant to Article 26 of the Rome Statute. The evidence and conclusion by Defence Child Soldier Expert, Major (ret) Pollar Awich, who himself was a formerly abducted child soldier by the National Resistance Army (NRA), later known as the Uganda Peoples' Defence Forces (UPDF), was totally rejected by the Chamber in the Trial Judgment.[8] In a blatant demonstration of racial and cultural legal biases underpinning its *Ongwen Exceptionalism*, the Chamber, in its Reparations Order, recognized the long-lasting consequences and harms of being a child soldier,[9] but rejected that Mr. Ongwen, a former child soldier, also suffered from these enduring effects and harms.[10]

The Appeals Chamber found a "shortcoming" in the reasoning of the Trial Chamber in rejecting Mr. Ongwen's appeal on substantially diminished mental capacity as a mitigating factor in sentencing but, without legal basis, found "no error irrespective of this shortcoming." By this reasoning, the Appeals Chamber carved out another "Ongwen Exception" with a new threshold of "shortcoming" which is permissible, as distinct from "error," which is sanctionable pursuant to Article 81 of the Rome Statute.[11]

---

[8] TJ, para. 612.

[9] Reparations Order, paras. 368–369, 414 (f) and (g).

[10] Reparations Order, para. 127.

[11] *Ongwen* Appeal Judgment on Sentence, para. 235: "Furthermore, the Trial Chamber noted that 'the evidence establishes clearly that at all relevant times for the charges, [Mr] Ongwen did not suffer from a mental disease or defect.' It also found that '[t]he evidence indicates that he was in full possession of his mental faculties and exercised his role as commander effectively.' The Appeals Chamber notes that the Trial Chamber's reasoning in this respect is rather brief. The Trial Chamber seems to have assumed that its conclusions made in the Conviction Decision were clear, such that there was no need to elaborate on why they were 'also incompatible with any consideration of substantially diminished mental capacity.' *It would have been preferable for the Trial Chamber to indicate with more detail precisely how it reassessed the evidence under the different standard of proof and in relation to the different threshold. However, the Appeals Chamber finds no error, irrespective of this shortcoming.*" (italics added)

Dominic Ongwen informed the Trial Chamber during the Sentencing Hearing on 15 April 2021 that since he surrendered to the ICC, he was not feeling well and that he did not consider himself human, especially concerning his mental health. Mr. Ongwen stated that despite the medical attention he was receiving to enable him to participate in his trial, he was able to understand only about 40% of the trial proceedings.[12]

During the Appeals Hearing on 18 February 2022, Mr. Ongwen informed the Appeals Chamber that due to his mental health disability, he was not able to follow the proceedings most of the time and that the only thing that was going on in his head was sounds of gunfire. Whenever he heard fireworks from his detention cell, he would start looking for his gun because the only thing that he knew was about guns. He dreams about guns and the only person who instructed him from an early age was Kony. "Nobody taught me anything else other than Kony." Mr. Ongwen likened his situation before the ICC to "a guinea fowl that was plucked out of the bush and put to live among chicken. I was like a caterpillar and now I'm turning into a butterfly."[13] The book captures this picture which Mr. Ongwen painted of his trial and about himself at the ICC succinctly.

The racial and cultural judicial biases against Mr. Ongwen were manifested in denying him a basic fair trial right of translating the evidence at trial into the language of the Court and into a language he understood. These judicial biases against Mr. Ongwen were compounded by a violation of Article 64(2) for all the 2507 items of evidence related to the interception of LRA radio communications by the Ugandan government through a bar table which it admitted as formally submitted over Defence objections, to be translated into the language of the Court and into a language which Mr. Ongwen understands, to enable the Court to fulfil the fair trial requirements of Article 64(2) of the Statute.

During the status conference at the commencement of this trial, the Defence requested the disclosure of the identity of individuals in intercepted audios which the Prosecution had disclosed and intended to use for the trial of Mr. Ongwen to enable the Defence to prepare its case. The

[12] T-261, pp. 3–4.

[13] T-267, pp. 35–36, 43–46.

Prosecution disclosed that the intercepts constituted about half of the Prosecution's case against Mr. Ongwen. The Prosecution opposed the Defence request but conceded that it did not know "about to whom a particular voice might belong."[14] During trial, the Chamber decided against the transcription and translation of the intercepted radio communications and disregarded the evidence altogether on the ground that it was not in the working language of the Court. By disregarding this evidence, the Chamber impermissibly failed to base its Judgment on an assessment of all the evidence in the trial record.[15]

For whatever it takes, a reasonable trier of fact would have ordered a translation of the audios into the language of the Court and a language Mr. Ongwen understood in order to fulfil the provisions of Article 64(2) of the Statute. These egregious violations could not have occurred in a case of a mentally disabled and mentally impaired child soldier from a European country or any other region of the world.

The Confirmation of Charges ("COC") Decision, dated 23 March 2016, containing the charges against Dominic Ongwen does not contain information about his background. The charges merely stated his status within the Lord's Resistance Army ("LRA") and that Joseph Kony, the undisputed leader, maintained a tight grip on the organization and also successfully invoked the possession of mystical powers. The Chamber did not carry out an assessment of the exercise of mystical powers by Joseph Kony on Dominic Ongwen and the conduct for which he was charged, even though this was central to the charges for which he stood trial. Indeed, the Chamber dismissed such analysis as unnecessary.

The book examines the Trial Chamber's consistent disregard of evidence of Acholi cultural factors, its spiritualism and traditional justice mechanisms. Evidence of *Mato Oput* was provided by Defence Experts, and complemented by evidence from *Ajwakas* (natural healers) and Acholi cultural leaders. The Chamber, instead, constructed an *Ongwen*

---

[14] T-25, p. 11, ll. 8–10.

[15] Audios of LRA intercepts provided by Prosecution witness P-0027 and Lt. Col. Timothy Kanyogonya, who was the chain of custody witness and the official liaison of the UPDF and the Government of Uganda with the OTP, were disregarded on the sole reason the evidence was in *a non-working language of the Court. See Ongwen* Trial Judgment, paras. 643, 650, 688, 690, 701, 710, 716, 722, 740,746, 753, 760,767,780, 782, 786,798, 804 (italics added).

crimes environment which was detached from the LRA crime environment, Joseph Kony and the cultural reality of the case. The book explores this point and the cultural judicial biases which informed the Chamber's decision.

This point in the book is supported by Prime Minister Ambrose Olaa of Ker Kwaro Acholi (KKA), the cultural institution of the Acholi people, in the following excerpt in a report he submitted to the Trial Chamber for consideration in the sentencing of Dominic Ongwen:[16]

> I do recognize the ICC as a multi-lateral institution established to dispense justice for war crimes around the world, upon which member nations sign up to. In our observation and outlook, the ICC bears both strengths and weaknesses. Its strength lies on its reliance on globally accepted legal standards and practices that define formal justice. Its weakness lies in its inability to contend with intricate, complex local realities and facts existing among distinct identities of the different societies it interacts with. It sets its own parameters, limits and boundaries and goes by them while dispensing justice. Like many formal justice institutions, the ICC path to securing justice and accountability for victims of crimes against humanity has apparent variation in definition and understanding between how the formal systems and informal local systems do define and understand justice and accountability. The reliance on logical inferences to come to conclusions sometimes becomes the bone of contention in the final dispensation of justice as many alternative facts lie elsewhere in the unconventional realms of human understanding for instance the influence of spirituality and divine intervention in the commission of war crimes and in the quest for justice and accountability respectively.
>
> It is my contention that justice ought to be meaningful and wholesome. I believe that justice is a breathing organ of society that is continuously evolving and prolific cases as that of Dominic Ongwen provide a unique opportunity to enrich the culture of justice for the greater good of humanity.

---

[16] The Report is titled "Where does conviction and sentencing of Dominic Ongwen Leave the Acholi Society? Snippets in deciphering the contradiction in the understanding of traditional Justice in Acholi in relation to the ICC judgment and eventual conviction of Dominic Ongwen." It was filed by the Defence as document number UGA-D26-0015-1812 in the case record, but was disregarded by the Trial Chamber, as were other reports which were filed by Acholi cultural leaders during Trial, Sentencing and the Reparations phases of the case.

> This opinion reiterates the above guiding principles and is not intended to undermine the processes and decisions of the ICC, including that on the judgment and sentencing of Dominic Ongwen.[17]

The population in the afflicted communities have over several years relied on the cultural mechanisms and cultural factors to rebuild their lives and to live together in peace and harmony. The racial and cultural justice biases which led to the rejection of these cultural factors undermined the very essence of justice. Particularly, denying Dominic Ongwen reasonable accommodation due to his mental health disability and a jaundiced lens in consideration and rejection of cultural factors due to racial and cultural judicial biases significantly impaired the credibility of the Judgment in the *Ongwen* case. By bringing the spotlight on this misjudgment, Beth S. Lyons has made a significant contribution to the development of international criminal justice.

[17] UGA-D26-0015-1813-1814.

1

If Black Were White: The Impact of Racial and Cultural Biases and Blindspots on the International Criminal Court's *Ongwen* Trial Judgment

Abstract Dominic Ongwen was abducted in 1987 by the Lord's Resistance Army ("LRA") in Northern Uganda when he was 8 or 9 years old and trafficked as a child soldier; he made multiple unsuccessful attempts to escape and finally succeeded in late 2014. He turned himself into the International Criminal Court in 2015. Mr. Ongwen was, and continues to be, a victim of Joseph Kony's Lord's Resistance Army. This chapter critiques the judicial racial and cultural biases and blindspots in the *Ongwen* Judgment, as related to the affirmative defences of mental disease or defect and duress, under Article 31 of the Rome Statute and to sentencing. These biases and blindspots prevented the Judges from assessing the evidence in an impartial manner and correctly applying the law to Mr. Ongwen's defences. My contention is that if the LRA were a

The author expresses her deepest gratitude and appreciation to Prof. Emilio Ovuga and Dr. Dickens Akena for generously sharing their knowledge with the *Ongwen* Defence Team. She is grateful to colleagues and the anonymous reviewer who read earlier versions of this chapter and provided suggestions and comments. These include Evelyn Ankumah, Evelyn Asaala, Tibor Bajnovic, Kamari Clarke, Mark Drumbl, Julie Fraser, Tom Maliti, Doireann McCarthy, Luke Moffett, Charles Nyankieya, Emilio Ovuga, Peter Robinson, Mimi Rosenberg, Emmett Simmons, Francis M. Ssekandi, Julius Sulmonetti, Charles A. Taku, Melinda Taylor and Lynne Wilson.

B. S. Lyons, *Race, Culture and Mental Illness in the International Criminal Court's Ongwen Judgment: Biases and Blindspots*, https://doi.org/10.1007/978-3-031-73683-4_1

predominantly white cult, or if it functioned in a predominantly white/ European country, or if the Defence Expert psychiatrists from Uganda were white or if the defendant, Mr. Dominic Ongwen, were white, the Trial Chamber would have reached a different conclusion about the affirmative defences of mental disease or defect and duress and acquitted him. For the International Criminal Court (ICC) to be a respected and legitimate organ of international justice, it must apply the rule of law to all and ensure fairness in its proceedings. This means, in part, confronting its racial and cultural biases and blindspots within its structure, as well as within the decisions and judgments which it renders.

Keywords Dominic Ongwen • Racial bias • Racism • White blindspot • Cultural bias • Culture • Blindspot • Affirmative defence • Article 31 (Rome Statute) • Duress • Mental illness • Mental disability blindspot • ICC • LRA • Child soldiers • Spiritualism • Acholi traditional justice • Selective prosecution • Sentencing

Introduction

If the Lord's Resistance Army were a predominantly white cult, if it functioned in a predominantly white/European country, if the Defence expert psychiatrists from Uganda were white or if the defendant, Mr. Dominic Ongwen, were white - would the Trial Chamber have reached a different conclusion about the affirmative defences of mental disease or defect and duress?

My answer is a resounding "yes."

If any *one* of these factors of whiteness existed, I contend that the Trial Judgment's approach and conclusions on the mental disease or defect and duress defences would have been favorable to Mr. Ongwen. The result would have been a finding that the Prosecution had not disproved the elements of the affirmative defences for excluding criminal responsibility under Article 31 (1)(a) and (d) beyond a reasonable doubt. Mr. Ongwen would have been acquitted.

This chapter critiques the judicial racial and cultural biases in the *Ongwen* Trial Judgment, as they relate to the affirmative defence of mental disease or defect under Article 31 (Grounds for excluding criminal responsibility) in the ICC's Rome Statute, and in the sentencing of Mr. Ongwen. These biases blinded the Judges and prevented them from assessing the evidence in an impartial manner and correctly applying the law. They were a significant factor in the Trial Chamber's rejection of Mr. Ongwen's affirmative defences, mental disease or defect and duress.

Chapter 1 is divided into two parts: Part 1 discusses racial and cultural bias and blindspots related to mental health issues; Part 2 discusses the role of spiritualism in the *Ongwen* case, and the impact of racial and cultural biases in sentencing. The final section in Part 2 asks: How can the ICC move forward on the issues of culture and race after *Ongwen*?

* * *

The *Ongwen* case is the most complex single-defendant case to date at the ICC. The numbers for everything are staggering:

- Mr. Ongwen was charged with 70 counts and 7 modes of liability and the Confirmation of Charges ('COC') decision was 104 pages;
- The *Ongwen* case has been in the ICC system for 17 years and counting: from the initial arrest warrant in 2005 through the Appeal Judgment in 2022, and it is currently in the Reparations Phase;
- The Trial Chamber issued a total of 663 decisions in various formats;[1]
- There were 5149 items recognized as formally submitted into evidence;[2]
- The Prosecution presented 116 witnesses; the Defence presented 63 witnesses;[3]
- The Trial Judgment is 1077 pages; the Appeal Judgment is 611 pages.

The *Ongwen* case is a case of many "firsts." It is the first ICC prosecution of a mentally disabled defendant who asserted the affirmative defences of mental disease or defect, and duress under Rome Statute, Article 31(1)(a) and (d) (grounds for excluding criminal responsibility) as

[1] Trial Judgment ('TJ'): 25.

[2] *Ibid.*, para. 25.

[3] *Ibid.*, para. 19.

complete defences.[4] It is the first case in which culture and spiritualism played a prominent role in the Defence. It is the first ICC prosecution of a defendant for crimes for which he is also a victim. And, to date, it the longest COC decision charging a single defendant, and the longest single defendant Trial Judgment[5] at the ICC.

But, this case was never about Mr. Ongwen; it was about the crimes of the LRA, directed by its leader, Joseph Kony. Mr. Ongwen was a scapegoat for the LRA's crimes—it is Joseph Kony who should have been sitting in the dock at the ICC. As Mr. Ongwen told the Trial Chamber at the opening of trial in December 2016:

> ...I'm not the LRA. The LRA is Joseph Kony who is the leader of the LRA... It is the LRA who abducted people in northern Uganda. The LRA killed people in northern Uganda. LRA committed atrocities in northern Uganda, and I'm one of the people against whom the LRA committed atrocities. But it's not me, Dominic Ongwen, personally, who is the LRA.[6]

On 19 January 2024, after Mr. Ongwen's 61 convictions for which he is serving a twenty-five year sentence, the Prosecution finally filed charges against Mr. Kony. Mr. Kony is alleged to have

> ...founded the LRA and was its military and political leader throughout the charged period [1 July 2002 to 31 December 2005], with overall authority and control over LRA members, including fighters participating in the charged crimes....KONY had the ultimate power to decide the fate of all LRA members, including senior commanders. Many members of the LRA believed he had spiritual power and was omniscient, beliefs which KONY perpetuated to exert control over the LRA.[7]

---

[4] Rome Statute, Article 31 at RS-Eng.pdf (icc-cpi.int).

[5] The Judgment is replete with errors, based in law, fact and procedure. Most of these errors are the denial of Mr. Ongwen's fair trial rights and the failure of the Trial Chamber to apply the burden of proof to the Prosecution, in respect to the affirmative defences, and in its assessments and conclusions about other evidence. *See*, *Prosecutor v. Ongwen*, ICC-02/04-01/15-1826 (May 21, 2021), Defence Notification of its Intent to Appeal the Judgment ('Defence Notification') at CR2021_04746.PDF (icc-cpi.int).

[6] T-26, p. 17, ll. 6, 10–14.

[7] Document Containing the Charges against Mr. Kony, CR2024_00006.PDF (icc-cpi.int), paras. 9–11.

The charged crimes against Mr. Kony cover the same temporal jurisdiction as Mr. Ongwen's convictions, and include the LRA attacks on four IDP camps (Pajule, Odek, Lukodi, Abok) for which Mr. Ongwen was convicted. In addition, Mr. Kony is charged with sexual and gender based crimes, and conscripting and using children in hostilities. A hearing for the Confirmation of Charges ('COC') in the *Kony* case is scheduled for 15 October 2024. The Pre-Trial Chamber II ruled, at the Prosecutor's request, that the hearing will proceed *in absentia*, if Mr. Kony fails to appear in Court.[8]

Mr. Ongwen was, and still remains, a victim of the LRA. He was never "transformed" into a perpetrator when he reached 18 years, the age of culpability in the ICC's Rome Statute, Article 26.[9] Mr. Ongwen suffered from mental diseases stemming from his initial abduction by the LRA which continue to plague him today, as he serves his sentence, now in Norway. Mr. Ongwen acted under duress in the LRA, "growing up" in its criminal environment where disobedience and escape were punishable with death or serious injury. Mr. Ongwen's deep spiritualism as an Acholi (and the spiritualism of other abductees) was abused by Joseph Kony for his own ends: to force child soldiers to commit heinous acts against each other and against the communities the LRA attacked, particularly in Northern Uganda.

* * *

The "Situation in Uganda," within which the *Ongwen* case is placed by the ICC, concerns events between 2002 and 2005, during the Government of Uganda's war against the LRA in Northern Uganda. But the ICC is prosecuting only one side of the conflict – the LRA. The well-documented crimes of the Uganda Peoples' Defence Forces (UPDF), during the Government's decades-long war against the LRA, including the time period of the charges in the *Ongwen* case (2002–2005), have never been investigated or prosecuted by the ICC. These crimes include forcing

[8] Information on the Kony case is available at Kony | International Criminal Court (icc-cpi.int). On 12 September 2024, Pre-Trial Chamber III decided to postpone the commencement of the Confirmation Hearing, scheduled for 15 October 2024.

[9] Rome Statute of the International Criminal Court (2011) at RS-Eng.pdf (icc-cpi.int).

populations into internally displaced persons (IDP) camps, resulting in a humanitarian crisis that has been described as a genocide in Northern Uganda.[10]

How did this selective prosecution happen? As part of its negotiations for the "self-referral" of the Uganda situation by the Museveni government in 2004, the ICC effectively guaranteed that the crimes of the UPDF during the civil war would not be investigated, and therefore, could not be prosecuted.[11] There was a *quid pro quo* – Uganda's "self-referral" to the ICC in exchange for no investigation of the UPDF crimes.

Selective prosecution as a policy was well-entrenched at the International Criminal Tribunal for Rwanda (ICTR), which was a court of "victor's justice": investigation and prosecution was reserved for only one-side of the conflict in 1994 - the "losing side" which no longer held State power. Although mandated by the General Assembly to investigate both sides of the 1994 conflict in Rwanda,[12] the ICTR selectively investigated and prosecuted only Hutu defendants. No members of the Rwandan Patriotic Front ('RPF') and no Tutsis were prosecuted. The Gersony Report, prepared by a UNHCR Emergency Repatriation Team led by Robert Gersony in August/September 1994, found that there were systematic killings of Hutus by the RPF's army, the Rwandan Patriotic Army ('RPA'), in 1994. These findings were presented to the Commission of Experts in October 1994, whose report concluded that

[10] Olara A. Otunnu (former UN Under Secretary-General and Special Representative for Children and Armed Conflict), *The Secret Genocide*, FOREIGN POLICY, October 19, 2009 at The Secret Genocide – Foreign Policy. *See also*, testimony of Prosecution witness Rwot Oywak, a Chief in Acholiland, who testified about the problems of hunger, disease, lack of freedom of movement in Pajule IDP camp and that "people did not go to the camps on their own volition" but because of government policies (T-81 at International Criminal Court (legal-tools.org, pp. 1–10); testimony of Defence Expert Dr. Adam Branch on forced displacement, the "wretched" conditions in the camps, and government policy of placing military soldiers and military barracks inside the camps, so that the LRA would have to attack civilians before reaching the Ugandan military at T-218 pdf (legal-tools.org); testimony of Defence Witness, Mr. Richard Otim, who lived in Pajule camp, describes how the Ugandan government asked everyone to move to the camps, but provided no assistance; that UPDF military barracks were as close as 100 metres to the camp; and soldiers were often in the camp to socialize and visit family, T-219, legal-tools.org/doc/e9a3e4/pdf/, pp. 5–10.

[11] Phil Clark, DISTANT JUSTICE, THE IMPACT OF THE INTERNATIONAL CRIMINAL COURT ON AFRICAN POLITICS, Cambridge University Press (2018), Chapter 3; *also see*, David Hoile, JUSTICE DENIED, THE REALITY OF THE INTERNATIONAL CRIMINAL COURT, Africa Research Center (2014), Chapters 10, 15.

[12] UNGA Res. 955 (November 8, 1994), Article 1 at S/RES/955(1994).

individuals from both sides of the conflict in Rwanda perpetrated serious breaches of international humanitarian law.[13]

In 2002–2003, a few years before the Uganda referral to the ICC, the former ICTR/ICTY Chief Prosecutor Carla Del Ponte initiated "Special Investigations" of the RPF crimes in 1994. Due to pressure from Rwanda,[14] her position as ICTR Chief Prosecutor was not renewed in 2003. The Report of RPF crimes during 1994[15] was submitted in October, 2003 to her successor, Chief Prosecutor Hassan Bubacar Jallow. But, no legal action was ever taken against the RPF by the ICTR. Investigations and prosecutions of the RPF crimes were "off limits." With the complicity of the ICTR, both the Kagame and Museveni governments were protected from the tentacles of the legal processes of international justice.

* * *

No justice was done in the *Ongwen* case. As two of the judges in the *Bemba* Appeal Judgment stated, "Justice can only be done when the right person is held responsible for the right charges, after a fair trial and on the

---

[13] These findings were supported by reports from Human Rights Watch as well as indictments and international arrest warrants filed by judges in Spain and France. In November 2006, French Judge Jean-Louis Bruguière issued an order for international arrest warrants for nine RPF leaders, charging them with being part of a terrorist enterprise involved in the planning and execution of the assassinations of two African Heads of State, President Juvenal Habyarimana of Rwanda and President Cyprien Ntaryamira of Burundi, and twelve other passengers and crew, in the shooting down of their plane on 6 April 1994, under the orders of President Paul Kagame. Judge Bruguière requested that the ICTR initiate legal proceedings against President Kagame for his presumed involvement in ordering and planning these assassinations.

In February 2008, Spanish Judge Andreu Merelles issued an indictment against forty RPF officials for crimes against humanity, war crimes, genocide and terrorism, from 1990 to 2002, against the civilian population, and primarily against members of the Hutu ethnic group. *See, The Spanish Indictment of High-ranking Rwandan Officials, by Commentator*, HeinOnLine, 6 J. INT'L CRIM. JUST. 1003 (2008) at pdf (legal-tools.org).

[14] *See*, "Del Ponte Says UN Caved to Rwandan Pressure," by Steven Edwards, September 17, 2003 at https://www.globalpolicy.org/component/content/article/163/29047.html; *See also*, Carla Del Ponte and Chuck Sudetic, MADAME PROSECUTOR, CONFRONTATIONS WITH HUMANITY'S WORST CRIMINALS AND THE CULTURE OF IMPUNITY, Other Press LLC (2009), Chapter 9.

[15] Report on Special Investigations of Crimes of the RPA in 1994, dated October 2003 at ictr-report-special-investigations-concerning-rpa-crimes.pdf (wordpress.com).

basis of robust evidence."[16] Dominic Ongwen was the wrong person, who wrongly faced, and was convicted of, charges that should have been prosecuted against Joseph Kony, in proceedings with a myriad of fair trial violations.[17]

Part 1: Mental Health Issues

Introduction

Part 1 identifies the judicial racial and cultural biases in the *Ongwen* case in the area of mental health, in the context of the Article 31 affirmative defence of mental disease or defect. It explores how the Trial Judgment's rejection of the Defence Experts' evidence is affected by such biases,[18] and how these biases directly impacted on its legal errors. I contend that the Chamber's biases on race and culture played a disproportionately significant role in its judicial decision-making. I am not arguing that these were the only factors operating in the Chamber's holdings, or that the Chamber intentionally disregarded the impact of race and culture in its conclusions. I also am not addressing *whether* race and culture played a role, but looking at *what* role they played.

It comes as no surprise that racial and cultural biases operated in the Trial Judgment. It is a "given" that racial and cultural biases permeate our society and seep into every crevice. They continue to poison institutions and individuals. Judicial institutions, such as the ICC, and judicial decision-makers, such as its judges, are not exempt or immune from these

---

[16] *Prosecutor v. Bemba*, ICC-01/05-01/08-3636-Anx2, Appeals Chamber, Separate Opinion Judge Van den Wyngaert and Judge Morrison, para. 78 (June 8, 2018) at CR2018_02989.PDF (icc-cpi.int).

[17] *See Prosecutor v. Ongwen*, ICC-02/04-01/15-1722-Corr-Red, Public Redacted Version of "Corrected Version of 'Defence Closing Brief,' filed on 24 February 2020," 13 March 2020, paras. 31–158 (Fair Trial and other Human Rights Violations), CR2020_00998.PDF (icc-cpi.int) ("DCB"); *Prosecutor v. Ongwen*, ICC-02/04-01/15-1866-Red Public Redacted Version of "Defence Appeal Brief Against the Convictions in the Judgment of 4 February 2021," filed on 21 July 2021 as ICC-02/04-01/15-1866-Conf (October 19, 2021) ("DAJ"), paras. 8–226 legal-tools.org/doc/b16rvj/pdf.

[18] *See*, DAJ, paras. 320–498 (Defence appeal of Article 31(1)(a) affirmative defence); paras. 433–450 (objections to cultural errors in the Trial Judgment).

biases.[19] Jeffrey J. Rachlinski and Sheri L. Johnson investigated whether judges hold implicit racial biases, and, if so, whether those biases produce biased judicial decisions.[20] Their study of implicit racial bias is based on 133 judges, recruited from different parts of the United States. They used the results of a Race IAT (Implicit Association Test) and hypothetical vignettes. They conclude that judges in the criminal justice system (like the rest of the population) hold implicit racial biases which can influence their judicial decisions. However, they also conclude that judges – if they are aware of, and knowledgeable about these biases - can exercise control over the influences of the biases, but this must be active and conscious control.[21] Hence, it is likely that when analyzing the legal conclusions in the *Ongwen* Trial Judgment, at least some implicit biases by the makers of these conclusions can be found in their reasoning. This is only logical.

The Rachlinski and Johnson study focused on individual judges "within the four corners of the courtroom." It is not clear, however, whether they were able to assess or measure the impact of the context in which the implicit biases are formulated and operate: a racist criminal justice system in a racialized U.S. The impact of systemic and structural racism in implicit bias is key – both in identifying the bias and in an individual's consciousness about the bias. Judges in national jurisdictions, as well as at the ICC, operate in a racialized world, not a "race-neutral" world, and this affects the justice they render in the courtroom.[22] It is this

---

[19] It is true, however, that individual Trial Chambers may approach mental health and culture differently. *See*, for example, *The Prosecutor v. Al Hassan Ag Abdoul Aziz Ag Mohamed Ag Mahmoud*, ICC-01/12-01/18 ("*Al Hassan*" case), where Trial Chamber X appointed an expert to the Panel of Experts ("POE") who was sensitive to cultural context and trauma resulting from torture. *See*, Decision appointing experts for the purpose of a medical examination pursuant to Rule 135 of the Rules of Procedure and Evidence, ICC-01/12-01/18-1006-Red 24-03-2021, paras. 9 and 32.

[20] Jeffrey J. Rachlinski and Sheri L. Johnson, *Does Unconscious Racial Bias Affect Trial Judges*, 84 NOTRE DAME L. REV. 1195 (2009), p. 1207. Available at: http://scholarship.law.nd.edu/ndlr/vol84/iss3/4.

[21] Rachlinski and Johnson distinguish between implicit and explicit bias: "by explicit bias, we mean the kind of bias that people knowingly – sometimes openly - embrace" and "implicit bias – by which we mean stereotypical associations so subtle that people who hold them might not even be aware of them…" p. 1196. *See also*, n. 39, *infra*.

[22] Randle C. DeFalco and Frédéric Mégret, *The invisibility of race at the ICC: lessons from the US criminal justice system*, 7(1) LOND. REV. INT. LAW, 55–87 (2019), p. 62 ("impoverished conceptualization of race and racism [viewing the ICC as race-neutral in a racialized world] has often led the Court to step into the trap of believing that an institution working in a deeply racialized world can nonetheless operate in a manner wholly emancipated from race and racism").

overall context of structural racism which supports the biases.[23] As a result of these implicit biases, the judges are prevented from assessing the evidence in an impartial manner and then correctly applying the law.

This chapter identifies how judicial biases related to race and culture are manifested in the *Ongwen* Trial Judgment,[24] and their implications for the implementation of international justice. Acknowledgment of the existence of these judicial biases is the predicate of any change. This is not simply a theoretical legal exercise: it affects how the ICC's decision in *Ongwen* is understood by those outside the confines of the ICC and whether the ICC is viewed as fair. Continuing to get race and culture issues wrong is not a viable option and leads to the illegitimacy of the ICC, its judgments and international justice.

This chapter addresses: Why did the Trial Chamber *not* find that evidence of Mr. Ongwen's affirmative defence of mental illness raised reasonable doubt in the Prosecution Experts' position, which was that Mr. Ongwen did not suffer from a mental disease or defect? Why did the Trial Chamber adopt an "all or nothing" approach to the Defence Experts' evidence? What went wrong in the Trial Chamber's analysis, which resulted in the wholesale rejection of the affirmative defences, particularly mental disease or defect, supported by the evidence of the Defence Experts, psychiatrists Prof. Emilio Ovuga ("Prof. EO") and Dr. Dickens Akena ("Dr. DA")? Why did the Chamber uncritically accept the evidence of the Prosecution Experts, especially Dr. Gillian Mezey ("Dr. GM") and Prof. Roland Weierstall-Pust ("Prof. W-P")?

---

[23] *See* Randle C. DeFalco and Frédéric Mégret, *supra*, p. 58 (ICC not immune particularly to structural racism and its "selective blindness to race may implicate ICC in the perpetuation of certain racist attitudes and beliefs clearly antithetical to its cosmopolitan anti-racist aspirations"); Rachel López, *Black Guilt, White Guilt at the International Criminal Court*, Black Guilt, White Guilt at the International Criminal Court by Rachel López : SSRN, 6 October 2022, in Matiangai V.S. Sirleaf ed., RACE AND NATIONAL SECURITY (Oxford University Press: New York 2023) ("…these [ICC] rules have criminalized the processes by which the Global North became wealthy, at the same time as effectively granting them *de facto* amnesty for those same acts"); Kamari Clarke, *Negotiating Racial Injustice: How International Criminal Law Helps Entrench Structural Inequality*, JUST. SEC. (July 24, 2020), https://www.justsecurity.org/71614/negotiating-racial-injustice-how-international-criminal-law-helps-entrench-structural-inequality/ (impact of white supremacy in Rome Statute provisions)

[24] I have focused on the Trial Chamber's Judgment; the Appeals Chamber repeats and bolsters the same arguments in its Appeal Judgment ('AJ')

The Intersection of Race and Culture in the *Ongwen* Judgment

That race and culture would be relevant to, and operate in a mental disease or defect defence should be expected. The impact of race and culture on mental health has long has long been a fundamental perspective within significant sections of the profession. More than half a century ago, Frantz Fanon identified the phenomenon of cultural racism and its manifestations as institutional racism, which is rooted in the political and social contexts and structures in which mental health systems operate. He addressed this in detail in his revolutionary analyses of the effects of colonialism on the mental health of the colonized, and the colonizers in Algeria in the period of the anti-colonialist war against the French in the late 1950s and early 1960s.[25] He discusses both individual mental health consequences as well as the systemic, institutional racism of the mental health system.

Institutional racism and its impact on adverse mental health outcomes in Black and other communities of color has been widely explored, for example, in Felicia Lazaridou's and Suman Fernando's work on cultural racism and mental health.[26] They discuss the conceptual overlap of race and culture and the need to deconstruct institutional racism within the mental health arena. As Suman Fernando points out, "When racism is implemented and practised through the institutions of society, often without people involved even being aware that they are being racist, it is called 'institutional racism.'"[27]

Even though race and culture are separate concepts and not fungible, they are – at the same time – not totally distinct. While racial and cultural biases may be expressed differently, it is difficult to draw a "bright

---

[25] *See* works of Frantz Fanon, including BLACK SKIN, WHITE MASKS (1952); THE WRETCHED OF THE EARTH (1961), A DYING COLONIALISM, (1959) and TOWARD THE AFRICAN REVOLUTION (1964) available from various publishers in French and English.

[26] *See*, Felicia Lazaridou and Suman Fernando, "Deconstructing institutional racism and the social construction of whiteness: A strategy for professional competence training in culture and migration mental health," 59(2) TRANSCULT. PSYCHIATRY (2022) 175–187 (discussion of cultural psychiatry).

[27] *See*, Suman Fernando, David Ndegwa and Melba Wilson, FORENSIC PSYCHIATRY, RACE AND CULTURE (London and New York: Routledge, 1998), p. 24.

red line" between them. One cannot parse out what is attributed exclusively to race and what is attributed exclusively to culture, because often there are no strict, immutable boundaries between the two.[28]

In the *Ongwen* Judgment, there are explicit discussions about culture, but the word "race" is not found. However, race is clearly in play in references to evidence discussing Africans and non-Africans. In addition, because of the "overlap" of culture and race, it could be argued that culture operates as a "code word" for race in the Judgment. The Trial Chamber's failure, for example, to encompass the Acholi traditional justice system within the principle of complementarity to ICC Western justice for Mr. Ongwen's sentence illustrates this point.[29] Its position demonstrates cultural bias, but also racial bias because the leaders in the Acholi traditional justice system and the persons in the communities which participate in it are Black.

The role of racial bias became prominent in the battle of the experts – particularly in the evidence of Prosecution Expert Prof. W-P, supported by Dr. GM (discussed *infra.*) and the Prosecution's treatment of the Defence Experts. During the Prosecution's cross-examination of the Defence Expert, Prof. Emilio Ovuga ('Prof. EO'), the senior prosecutor accused Prof. EO of suggesting "nonsense."[30] After being rebuked by the Trial Chamber, Defence Counsel and the witness, the Prosecutor promptly apologized that he was out of order and used hypoglycemia as an excuse. The absurdity of the Prosecutor's "explanation" highlights the question of why the Prosecutor felt he had license to disrespect the Defence Expert witness. It raises the question: would the Prosecutor have thought twice before he accused the Defence Expert of uttering "nonsense" if the Defence Expert were white, and not Black? If he were white, the Prosecution still may have aggressively cross-examined him, but <u>without</u> the disrespect displayed in the ICC courtroom. Whether the

[28] While earlier work of Fernando distinguishes between race and culture, he and Lazaridou discuss the overlap or intersection of these concepts in the notion of cultural racism in 2022 article at n.26.

[29] Discussed *infra* in Chap. 1, Part 2.

[30] T-251, pp. 31–34 at CR2019_07320.PDF (icc-cpi.int); DCB, paras. 611–615; DAJ, para. 372, n.423. *See*, https://www.ijmonitor.org/2020/02/senior-prosecutor-comes-under-criticism-for-calling-defense-witnesss-testimony-nonsense/ Only one of the *amici*, Justice Francis Muzingu Ssekandi, notes that the Prosecutor characterized Prof. EO's opinions as "nonsense." *Amicus Brief*, ICC-02/04-01/15-1926 20-12-2022, para. 21.

Prosecutor's conduct in this example is categorized as unconscious, or implicit or unspoken bias – its effect is the same.

* * *

The Judgment's cultural and racial biases have resulted in (at least) two fundamental legal errors: (a) the failure to apply the beyond a reasonable doubt standard and (b) a disintegration of evidentiary standards of credibility and reliability. These errors resulted in harms to Mr. Ongwen as the defendant who was convicted, and - at the global level - are key indicia of a more endemic crisis – the legitimacy of international justice. The question is: Will the impact of culture and race be recognized and taken into account in international judicial proceedings and jurisprudence?

First, the Judgment rejected the mental disease defence and took an "all or nothing" approach to the Defence Experts' evidence. By "all or nothing approach," I mean that the Trial Chamber completely and unequivocally rejected every piece of evidence from the Defence Experts. The Chamber credited nothing from the Defence Experts. Conversely, it credited practically all of the Prosecution Experts' evidence and, simplistically, accepted (lack of mental illness) diagnoses, even though these were premised on highly contested theories within the mental health profession. For example, the idea proposed by the Prosecution Experts Prof. W-P and Dr. GM and held in the Judgment was that a person with post-traumatic stress disorder (PTSD) is dysfunctional all the time, 24/7; since Mr. Ongwen "rose in the ranks" of the LRA, he was functional and could not be suffering from PTSD.[31] Thus, *nothing* in the Defence Experts' evidence raised a reasonable doubt in the Chamber's mind. I am not sure, moreover, that the Chamber was even looking at whether the Defence Experts' evidence raised reasonable doubt in the Prosecution testimony. I conclude this since the term "reasonable doubt" hardly appears in the Judgment as the standard against which the evidence is assessed.[32] The Defence argument was that the Chamber, although it articulated the correct burden of proof beyond a reasonable doubt on the Prosecution,

[31] *See*, DCB, paras. 637–650; TJ: 2461–2557; DAJ, paras. 362–363, 387.

[32] DAJ, para. 200 (Trial Chamber makes only one finding re evidence and reasonable doubt).

failed to apply this burden in reaching its conclusions.[33] Its fundamental error was the failure to apply reasonable doubt in assessing the Defence Experts' evidence while accepting the Prosecution Experts' evidence, especially that of Prof. W-P. In doing so, the Chamber failed to express any caution or acknowledge the impact of racial and cultural biases on its analysis, or the decades-long ongoing debate within the profession. Thus, the Trial Chamber's analysis and conclusions gave no legal weight to the beyond a reasonable doubt standard.

These cultural and racial biases prevented the Judges from concluding that the Defence Experts' evidence raised reasonable doubt. The judicial biases meant that the Judges did not see, for example, that cultural factors affected their views that psychometric testing was useful in all cultures in mental health assessments, or that lay witness observations were not undermined by the LRA environment in which the witnesses lived. These biases obstructed the analytical process – and the Judges disregarded and discounted factors relevant to the evidence. Had these judicial biases not been operating, then Mr. Ongwen's affirmative defences would have prevailed, and he would have been acquitted.

Second, the Trial Chamber played "fast and loose" with its assessment of the evidentiary criteria of credibility and reliability. It concluded that <u>none</u> of the evidence of the Defence Experts was reliable.[34] The term "credible" was not used in the Trial Judgment in its sections about the Defence Experts' evidence. In contrast, both terms—reliable and credible—were used in its analysis of the fact witnesses in the Judgment, and it appears that they were used almost interchangeably.[35] This could lead to the conclusion that it is difficult to distinguish between reliable versus credible evidence. But, in any case, it raises the question as to why, in the very beginning, neither the Prosecution nor the Court, *sua sponte*, challenged the Defence Experts when they were proposed as Defence Experts.

---

[33] In a criminal trial, the burden of proof beyond a reasonable doubt (BRD) is on the Prosecution. *See*, TJ: 231. The Trial Chamber's error was that it did not apply this to the affirmative defences and did not articulate the legal standard or burden of proof re affirmative defences during trial. The Defence position is that when applied to affirmative defences, the Prosecution's burden is *to disprove each and every element of the affirmative defence beyond a reasonable doubt. See*, DCB, paras. 91–96; DAJ, paras. 198–219 (TJ errors re legal standards and burden of proof).

[34] TJ: 2574.

[35] *See* witness testimonies summarized in Trial Judgment.

Rather, both Prof. EO and Dr. DA were accepted as Experts, and their report was entered into evidence, without a whisper of an objection. Why was the Defence Experts' methodology not attacked at this initial stage? Why did the Prosecution wait? Why did the Chamber appear to reverse its position on the Defence Experts, whom it had accepted but who were now transformed into "unreliable witnesses"?

There is an assumption that professional judges in international courts and tribunals rigorously scrutinize their findings and conclusions of fact and law for consistency in their judgments. Applying this to *Ongwen,* how did the Trial Chamber end up with the "all or nothing" approach? Was there "something else" which made it impossible for the Trial Chamber to act *consistently* with its own espoused legal principles?

The Operation of Judicial Biases and Blindspots

I posit that the "something else" which interfered with the Trial Chamber's application of the law was a "blindspot," based on racial and cultural biases. This is reflected in the "all or nothing approach" to the mental illness evidence, in lieu of the correct standard of proof beyond a reasonable doubt.

In addition, the Trial Chamber's failure to reasonably accommodate Mr. Ongwen's mental disability was buttressed by a "mental disability blindspot."[36] Discussed more fully in Chap. 2, I argue that the Chamber had a "mental disability blindspot" because it did not recognize Mr. Ongwen's mental disability, based on his traumas as a child soldier as well as his diagnosed mental illnesses. This resulted in its failure to reasonably accommodate his disability in a timely fashion, and violation of his fair trial rights: for example, the Chamber's refusal to assess Mr. Ongwen's

[36] The Defence argued that the Trial Chamber erred in law and in fact in its conclusion that it did not discriminate against Mr. Ongwen, based on mental disability. *See*, DCB, paras. 79, 128; TJ: 73–80, 106–115; DAJ, paras. 69–76, 247–255; AJ: 164–220 (illegal plea); 422–450.

Rule 135 (RPE) Medical examination of the accused, states:

1. The Trial Chamber may, for the purpose of discharging its obligations under article 64, paragraph 8 (a), or for any other reasons, or at the request of a party, order a medical, psychiatric or psychological examination of the accused, under the conditions set forth in rule 113 at RulesProcedureEvidenceEng.pdf (icc-cpi.int).

mental health before the plea proceeding in December 2016, and a later denial of a Rule 135 request for a psychiatric examination, which prevented Mr. Ongwen from exercising his fair trial right to decide whether or not to testify in his own defence.

All of these biases and blindspots – racial, cultural, mental disability – are interrelated, although the expression and resulting harms of each may differ, depending on context.

(1) The notion of blindspot

The idea of "blindspot" is that it prevents one from seeing (and understanding) something: it may be a blindspot while driving which prevents the driver from seeing an oncoming vehicle at an intersection; it may mean that someone simply omits a category or factor in her or his thinking or analysis. The point is that blindspots obstruct full vision—both physically and mentally. This is detrimental not only to an outcome or result but also to the person with the blindspot.

I first learned about the "white blindspot" as a student activist in the 1960s in the United States.[37] The divisiveness of biases and blindspots, both conscious but especially unconscious, has informed my analytical

[37] In the 1960s, I was introduced to the term "white blindspot" by Ted Allen, *see* Theodore W. Allen, *Can White Workers [crossed out] Radicals be Radicalized*? at White blindspot: The original essays on combating white supremacy and white-skin priviledge, ca. 1969 (umass.edu). The concept was that white workers (in the U.S.) could not make common cause with black workers until they recognized their white blindspot and renounced their white-skin privilege. This blindspot was nurtured by the privileges bestowed on white workers, at the expense of Black workers: these privileges included rights of seniority, more pay for the same work, higher job classifications, and so on. White workers were held back from struggling fully for better working conditions because the employer would use the threat of Black workers working for less, or breaking a picket line. This was essentially the familiar "divide and conquer" scenario—where both Black and white workers were impacted by the blindspot, although the impact was unequal based on race. *See also*, W.E.B. DuBois, BLACK RECONSTRUCTION IN AMERICA 1860–1880 (New York: Atheneum, 1969), p. 577 (describing the contributions and accomplishments of Black people during Reconstruction, DuBois concludes "…[I]t is only the Blindspot in the eyes of America, and its historians, that can overlook and misread so clear and encouraging a chapter of human struggle and human uplift."); *also see* Theodore W. Allen, THE INVENTION OF THE WHITE RACE, VOL 1: RACIAL OPPRESSION AND SOCIAL CONTROL, Verso (1994 and 2021); VOL II: THE ORIGINAL OF RACIAL OPPRESSION IN ANGLO-AMERICA, Verso (1997, 2012).

approach generally.[38] When I use the term blindspot (whether white, Western or mental disability blindspot) in respect to the courts - in particular, the ICC and international criminal tribunals - it is shorthand for a fundamental factor that obstructs the court from dispensing justice in an equal and fair manner, effectively delegitimizing its authority.

(2) **Identifying and discussing biases**

Biases and blindspots do not exist in a vacuum. They reflect the racial-cultural-social-political-economic contexts that shape the power relations within a society. A complete analysis of how biases and blindspots operate includes a discussion of these contexts, but this is beyond the scope of this book.

Biases are the fodder of blindspots. Biases can be categorized as implicit or explicit, unconscious or intentional. But the nature of biases is that they are not necessarily forthright (explicit bias), and are often "hidden" or "under cover" (implicit bias).[39] Most people do not walk around with a sign that says they have a bias. There are no explicit admissions in the Judgment that say "culture or race do not count." So, one has to sift through the layers that may cover up these biases.

Biases also can co-exist with apparent non-biases: someone can exhibit a bias, then say or do the "right or politically correct thing."[40] But this

---

[38] I was surprised to find - almost half a century later - that a book entitled BLINDSPOT, HIDDEN BIASES OF GOOD PEOPLE, Bantam (2013) by Mahzarin R. Banaji and Anthony G. Greenwald was a *New York Times* bestseller in 2016. The book, using the blindspot on the retina which affects visual perception as a metaphor, focuses on a different blindspot: one with hidden biases or "mind-bugs" which are revealed in the Race Implicit Association Test (IAT) and interpreted by the authors. The authors analyze previous research on racial and ethnic bias, and includes a series of tests for the reader to take; they also discusses implications for gender and other biases and blindspots. The authors, with Brian Nosek, founded Project Implicit https://implicit.harvard.edu/

[39] Based on their studies, Banaji and Greenwald concluded that explicit bias in respect to race is infrequent, but implicit bias is pervasive (BLINDSPOT, p. 208). But, both result in discrimination, based on race, in all spheres of life, including the criminal justice system.

[40] The Trial Chamber's response to the Prosecutor's "nonsense" comment, *supra* at n.30, demonstrates its capacity to act fairly under some circumstances, but this does not make it immune or exempt from biases in other situations.

In addition, both Prof. W-P and Dr. GM acknowledged that culture impacts on mental health, and Dr. GM mentioned cultural psychiatry in her evidence and testified that she worked with people from many different cultures. But these are not "credentials" which make either expert immune from cultural bias, as discussed *infra*. *See*, Ana Antic, *Transcultural Psychiatry: Cultural*

does not cancel the bias – it just means that human beings sometimes operate inconsistently.

The racial and cultural biases to which I refer in the *Ongwen* Judgment are both implicit and explicit. Whether my categorization in the world of biases is scientifically accurate, and whether this matters, is for other experts to determine. My only point is that both categories operate in the *Ongwen* Judgment. My objective is not to determine unequivocally into which category the Chamber's judicial biases fit, but to address their ultimate result: the rejection of Mr. Ongwen's affirmative defences and its conclusions that he was guilty.

Michelle Alexander discusses the implicit and explicit biases against Black people in the United States government's War on Drugs. She points out that cognitive research demonstrates that even if a person does not intend to discriminate, both conscious and unconscious biases can lead to discriminatory actions.[41] Banaji and Greenwald conclude, based on studies of "America's persisting racial bias," that hidden biases contribute more to racial discrimination than overt, explicit biases.[42] But both categories of biases raise the issue of what role does intent, or - in the case of *Ongwen* – racial or cultural *animus* play, if any, in identifying biases? Or, is intent less of a factor, or not a factor all, in analyzing the results of bias, including discrimination?

Finding and rooting out bias is not an exact science, including in the case of judicial biases. Bias is hard to discern and—when identified—may be difficult to prove. One may find indicators of bias, or possible bias, but definitive bias may be more elusive. In a legal context, this can border on speculation and is "counter-intuitive" to the notions of legal standards and evidentiary proof in a trial. I do not think that this diminishes the value of identifying judicial biases or negates their existence. But

Difference, Universalism and Social Psychiatry in the Age of Decolonisation, 45 CULT. MED. PSYCHIATRY (2021), 359–384. Antic discusses examples of racism in the conceptualization of cultural psychiatry. She points out that there is a political spectrum of views on cultural psychiatry and that the more progressive interpretations come from Marxist psychiatrists in Eastern Europe, as well as from African and Asian psychiatrists.

[41] Michelle Alexander, THE NEW JIM CROW, MASS INCARCERATION IN THE AGE OF COLORBLINDNESS, The New Press (10th Anniversary Edition, 2020), pp. 130–137.

[42] Banaji and Greenwald, p. 187.

it certainly can make it more difficult to articulate how a bias shows itself, and its effect or result.

Any discussion of judicial biases has a subjective component. Regardless of how many times one re-iterates that a critique of the results of biases is objective, or that intent is excised from the equation, bias is still personal. Biases do not exist "in the abstract" or "on their own." Biases are held by people and, when acted upon, result in decisions that affect other people. So, when one is talking about racial and cultural judicial biases, they may result in or affect particular decisions and judgments. But these biases are coming from the persons, in this case, the Judges, who make the decisions and render the judgments.

However, it is important to remove the element of intent from the equation: I am not saying that the ICC or individual judges in the *Ongwen* Trial Chamber intended to discriminate against defendants of color, or mentally disabled defendants. I am obviously not privy to the Chamber's analytical processes during deliberations and I will not speculate. But, there are obstacles in the judicial arena which objectively encourage positions and practices that reflect racial and cultural biases, and biases related to mental disability. For example, the detrimental effect of a white blindspot means that the judges cannot fully understand and appreciate how the factor of race may be operating, both overtly and covertly, in their approach. The judicial responses may reflect implicit racial bias, and result in racially biased jurisprudence.

One key example of racial and cultural bias operating together is found in the Judgment's critique of the Defence Experts' methodology, where it emphasizes their failure to use psychometric testing for malingering, based on Prof. W-P's evidence. Within the mental health profession, psychometric testing has been widely criticized for decades for its cultural bias, and its applicability to, or use in non-Western societies has been challenged.[43] Despite this, the Trial Chamber failed to even acknowledge this cultural critique as a predicate issue and ignored the debate within the profession, rendering its own conclusions culturally biased. Objectively, this means that the Western blindspot prevented the Trial Chamber from applying the correct legal principle in assessing whether

[43] *See*, section on Cultural Bias and Scientific Standards, Psychometric Testing and Malingering, *infra*.

the Prosecution had met its burden of proof. If the Trial Chamber had not been "blinded," it likely would have considered the cultural limitations on using psychometric testing as the only tool for assessing malingering and then would not have simply adopted the culturally biased evidence of Prof. W-P without a *caveat* or caution.

How the Trial Chamber Handled the Mental Disease or Defect Affirmative Defence

(1) **Summary of the Trial Chamber's position**

The Judgment held that Mr. Ongwen did not suffer from a mental disease or defect which destroyed his capacity to appreciate that his conduct was unlawful, or to control his unlawful conduct (Article 31(1)(a)).[44] It also concluded that Mr. Ongwen did not suffer duress, as per Article 31(1)(d). In sum, the Trial Chamber rejected both affirmative defences for excluding criminal responsibility.

At trial, the Trial Chamber was presented with conflicting expert evidence on whether Mr. Ongwen's criminal responsibility should be excluded based on mental disease and duress. On one side were the Prosecution Experts—Dr. Gillian Mezey, Prof. Weierstall-Pust and Dr. Catherine Abbo—who concluded that Mr. Ongwen did not suffer from mental illness.[45] On the other side, there were the Defence Experts—Prof. Emilio Ovuga and Dr. Dickens Akena—as well as the Court-Appointed Expert, Prof. Joop de Jong—who concluded the opposite, that Mr. Ongwen did suffer from mental illnesses. The Defence Experts diagnosed Mr. Ongwen with the following mental diseases: in their First Report, they identified severe depressive illness, PTSD and dissociative disorder (including depersonalization and multiple identity disorder) as

[44] TJ: 2448–2580; AJ: 1105–1384.

[45] *See* TJ: 2450–2580 (evidence from Prosecution, Defence and Court-Appointed Experts); *also see*, DCB, paras. 535–674; DAJ, paras. 270–276, 320–419, 430–498.

well as severe suicidal ideation and high risk of committing suicide.[46] In their Second Report, they identified dissociative amnesia and symptoms of obsessive-compulsive disorder.[47] They concluded that Mr. Ongwen's mental illnesses stemmed from his forced abduction by the LRA around 1987, continued through his years in the LRA and still plague him today.[48]

The Court-Appointed Expert, Prof. de Jong, who was tasked with determining Mr. Ongwen's mental state at the time of the beginning of the trial, generally agreed with the conclusions of the Defence Experts. Prof. de Jong found that Mr. Ongwen suffered from severe depressive illness, PTSD and dissociative disorders.[49] For this reason, he was treated by the Prosecution and the Trial Judgment essentially as a Defence Expert.[50]

The affirmative defences related to mental disease and duress were the core of the Defence case and were argued as complete defences to all 70 charges (and seven modes of liability)[51] against Mr. Ongwen. The Defence, before it presented its case, requested that the Trial Chamber articulate the legal standard for affirmative defences, within the framework of the Prosecution's onus of proof beyond a reasonable doubt.[52] The Defence's position was that the Chamber had the legal obligation to apply the reasonable doubt standard and hold the Prosecution to its burden to prove Mr. Ongwen's guilt beyond a reasonable doubt. The Defence proposed the formulation that the Prosecution had the burden to disprove each and every element of the affirmative defence beyond a

[46] First Report, UGA-D26-0015-0004, pp. 12, 14–15.

[47] Second Report, UGA-D26-0015-0948, pp. 24–25.

[48] Second Report, UGA-D26-0015-0948, pp. 23–27 (noting, for example, chronic exposure to life-threatening traumatic experiences from 1986; hospitalization in Juba for mental illness after battle in 1997, incidents of loss of consciousness reported in 1996, 1997, 1999 and 2002).

[49] Prof. de Jong Expert Report, UGA-D26-0015-0046-R01, pp. 5–6 (p. 0051–0052).

[50] *See* AJ: 1278–1288, affirming the Trial Judgment's holdings on Prof. de Jong's evidence, and developing the Trial Chamber's arguments more fully.

[51] Appeals Chamber Decision, ICC-02/04-01/15-1562 17-07-2019, para. 14.

[52] DCB, paras. 91–96, 529–534; DAJ, paras. 198–215.

reasonable doubt, but this was explicitly rejected by the Chamber.[53] Nevertheless, throughout the trial, the Chamber did not articulate the legal standard for affirmative defences. In the Judgment, the Chamber cited proof beyond a reasonable doubt,[54] but did not explain how it worked in the case of an affirmative defence and did not apply it to the *Ongwen* case. In fact, in the whole Judgment, the Chamber only articulated the standard of proof beyond a reasonable doubt once, in reference to assessing evidence of intercepted audio recordings.[55]

The Trial Chamber rejected all the Defence Experts' and Court-Appointed Expert's evidence to reach its ultimate conclusion that Mr. Ongwen did not suffer from a mental disease or defect. Its rejection of the Defence Experts' evidence was based on the Chamber's conclusion that they had used faulty or deficient methodology, which rendered their conclusions unreliable. For the Court-Appointed Expert, the Judgment states that his report had been requested for the purpose of assessing Mr. Ongwen's current mental state at the time of the trial, and not for the purpose of assessing his mental state at the time of the charged crimes. Therefore, the Chamber did not rely on the diagnoses for Mr. Ongwen's mental status during the charged period.[56] The report included a history which Prof. de Jong obtained from Mr. Ongwen during clinical interviews, and was relevant in understanding Mr. Ongwen's current mental state at the time the report was prepared. However, the Chamber dismissed any historical assessments for its deliberations. On its face, this demonstrates that the Chamber had a scientifically unsound idea of how mental illness operates and did not understand the importance of an historical timeline in the evaluation, diagnosis and treatment of mental illness.

---

[53] At the appeal stage, the Appeals Chamber sought the opinion of 19 *amici curiae* on both affirmative defences, and other legal issues. *See*, Order inviting expressions of interest as *amici curiae* in judicial proceedings (pursuant to rule 103 of the Rules of Procedure and Evidence), ICC-02/04-01/15-1884 (Oct. 25, 2021).

[54] TJ: 226–231.

[55] TJ: 656.

[56] TJ: 2576–2578.

(2) The Trial Judgment's rejection of the Defence Experts' evidence based on methodology[57]

The Trial Chamber's conclusions were based on the premise that faulty methodology yields faulty conclusions.[58] It concluded that because the Defence Experts' methodology was faulty and deficient, none of their conclusions were credible or reliable.

The Trial Chamber cited six reasons, based principally on arguments from Prof. W-P's ("P-447") Rebuttal Report, to discredit and dismiss the Defence Experts' evidence. The factors raised by the Trial Chamber were:

#1: Blurring of role of Defence Experts (whether treating or forensic psychiatrists)[59]
#2: Failure of Defence Experts to apply "scientifically validated methods and tools"[60]
#3: Unexplained contradictions between observations and final conclusions of the Defence Experts[61]
#4: Defence Experts failed to use other resources or collateral information to corroborate conclusions[62]
#5: Explanations for excluding malingering were not satisfactory to the Trial Chamber[63]
#6: Defence reports are general and not focused on relevant period of charges[64]

---

[57] There is also an argument that if the judicial critique is only, or principally, about methodology, then judges do not have to do any "deep dives" into the DSM (DIAGNOSTIC AND STATISTICAL MANUAL OF MENTAL DISORDERS, 5th Edition, American Psychiatric Association) or ICD (International Classification of Diseases, World Health Organization), or Medline data bases, or professional journals. Critiques of methodology or process may be within the legal "comfort zone" of judges: these do not require them to decide whether a substantive mental condition exists. A "methodology first (and only)" approach solves the problem.

[58] TJ: 2535. *See*, DCB, paras. 651–653; DAJ, paras. 323–328, 342–353.

[59] TJ: 2528–2531.

[60] TJ: 2532–2535.

[61] TJ: 2536–2544.

[62] TJ: 2545–2557.

[63] TJ: 2558–2568.

[64] TJ: 2569–2573.

These "methodology criteria" illustrate the role of implicit racial and cultural biases in the Chamber's criteria on which it based its conclusions. In its pleadings, especially its Closing Brief and Appeal Brief, the Defence refuted each of the six factors. The Defence objected to the Trial Chamber's factual misrepresentations and legal contortions with which it deemed the Defence Experts' evidence unreliable.[65]

The Judgment's "methodology critique" communicates a (not so) veiled criticism that the Defence Experts are incompetent and unqualified and should not be regarded as experts. The Trial Chamber's critique of methodology is a critique of how the Defence Experts practice as psychiatrists and how they report on their findings as experts in a trial. It is a critique of their working methods and work-product as professionals, but this critique is also personal because it is nearly impossible to separate out the "person" from the "professional conduct."

The Judgment's critique has repercussions beyond the confines of the ICC. In essence, it is very much an unwarranted and unjustified public rebuke. The Defence Experts' testimony was a public event: both gave evidence over a period of almost two weeks in the Defence case, as well as in the Rebuttal Case. Media outlets in Uganda, Europe and elsewhere reported on their testimony.

In the *Ongwen* case, the critique of the Defence Experts' evidence as unreliable echoes the same racial bias and racism which exists when persons of color are too often labelled as "unqualified" for a job or a promotion and are discriminated against based on race.[66] The same person, however, in a situation where information about her or his race is not provided, would be considered qualified.

The factor of race is often revealed in the choice of language used to describe or characterize persons or events, in the context of crime. For example, Lazaridou and Fernando discuss how whiteness affects the portrayal of mental health and crime: a white shooter is described as

[65] DCB, paras. 604–674; DAJ (Grounds of appeal 27, 29, 31, 32, 35–41), paras. 320–419 – Factor #1 is refuted at paras. 329–341; Factor #2 at paras. 342–353; Factor #3 at paras. 354–372; Factor #4 at paras. 373–392; Factor #5 at paras. 393–409; Factor #6 at paras. 410–419.

[66] *See* BLINDSPOT, Appendix 2, p. 206 (where Black and white applicants are equally qualified for job or housing, white applicants receive favorable outcomes about twice as often as Black applicants).

"mentally ill," whereas a Black shooter has a dangerous (aka criminal) personality.[67]

The factor of race also pervades "scientific findings" on crime. Dror et al. conclude that race affects cognitive biases of forensic pathologists, for example, in determining whether a death is an accident or homicide—in the circumstances of a child brought to a hospital by a caregiver.[68] Where the white child is brought in by a grandmother, and where the Black child is brought in by the mother's boyfriend, pathologists were more likely to rule "homicide" rather than "accident" for deaths of Black children relative to white children. The study found that with identical medical data, forensic pathologists were biased in their decisions. It states:

> The data do not allow us to ascertain whether they were biased by the race of the child or/and characteristics of the caregiver. The important finding is that *their decisions were noticeably affected by medically irrelevant contextual information* (information that should not have any bearing on the decision).[69] (*italics* in original)

The race of the Defence Experts, both of whom are Black Ugandans, was never articulated as a factor by the Trial Chamber in reaching its conclusions. But, it becomes an issue in the Chamber's choice and application of criteria for methodology. This is compounded by the Chamber's failure to acknowledge even a possibility that its biases influenced its conclusion that the Defence Experts' evidence is unreliable, based on its deficient methodology. The unarticulated biases of the Chamber make its position on reliability of the evidence even more suspect, given that the Chamber

---

[67] Lazaridou and Fernando, *supra* at n.26, p. 178.

[68] *See*, Itiel Dror, Judy Melinek, Jonathan L Arden, Jeff Kukucka, Sarah Hawkins, Joye Carter, Daniel S. Atherton, *Cognitive bias in forensic pathology decisions*, 66(5) J. FORENSIC SCI., 20 February 2021, 1751–1757, Figure 3. Although the sampling was small (133 forensic pathologists), it found that race and implicit bias are factors in decision-making. *Also see*, Douglas Starr, *The Bias Hunter*, 376 (6594) SCIENCE, 12 May 2022; Janis C. Puracal, *The Role of Implicit Racial Bias in Forensic Testimony*, THE CHAMPION (July 2021) (online journal of National Association of Criminal Defense Lawyers [NACDL.org]) (implicit bias in forensic testimony is an "undeniable barrier to racial justice and equity...the question is, given that racial bias can be unintended and can persist hidden from view, what have labs or examiners done to protect their opinions from contamination, just as the labs would protect any other piece of evidence?")

[69] *Ibid.*, Dror et al. Section 5.

had accepted the expert status of both Defence Experts, as well as their reports, with no objection from the Prosecution.

The professional credentials of the Defence Experts were beyond reproach.[70] Collectively, they represented decades of leadership in psychiatry, both in academia and as practitioners, especially in forensic psychiatry, as well as other areas – which was recognized in Uganda and internationally. Most importantly, except for Prof. de Jong in late 2016 to early 2017 and the Detention Center professionals, the Defence Experts were the only psychiatrists to have interviewed Mr. Ongwen multiple times since 2016. They were familiar with the specifics of the Uganda situation and the war between the Government of Uganda and the LRA. They had lived through the time period of the crimes charged to Mr. Ongwen, and one of the Experts had a family member who had been killed by the LRA. Dr. DA, who hailed from the same region as Mr. Ongwen, testified that he knew the places Mr. Ongwen talked about, and he could have been in Mr. Ongwen's shoes: "I have lived in some of those places…But I also looked at the client and his age, and I looked back at that time and…this could have actually been me."[71]

The only Prosecution Expert who did not criticize the methodology of the Defence Experts in her evidence was Dr. Catherine Abbo, a Ugandan psychiatrist, who also testified about the importance of cultural psychiatry. She disagreed with the Defence Experts' conclusions and supported the Chamber's ultimate finding that Mr. Ongwen suffered no mental disease. But her evidence indicated that she understood the effects of the LRA's adverse environment on Mr. Ongwen and the continuing effects of trauma on mental health over long periods of time. She testified "…I would like to look at it on a timeline and not divorce Mr. Ongwen from his childhood because Mr. Ongwen did not fall from space as an adult. He grew up to adulthood from his childhood, so it becomes a little bit difficult for me to just say, Mr. Ongwen as an adult and Mr. Ongwen as a child because it's a continuous thing."[72] This was echoed by Raphael

[70] *See*, CV of Prof. Emilo Ovuga (UGA-D26-0015-0856) and CV of Dr. Dickens Akena (UGA-D26-0015-0849).

[71] *See*, DCB, para. 605 and T-248-Red, p. 42, l. 8 - p. 43, l. 2.

[72] Testimony of Dr. Abbo, T-166, pp. 55, ll. 22–25 to p. 56, l.1. *See also* DAJ, paras. 484–486 (support of this position by Court-Appointed Expert Prof. de Jong at n.559).

Pangalangan, who wrote that "…Ongwen, the Brigadier General, carries with him the same traumas and values formed by Ongwen the child soldier."[73] In addition, Dr. Abbo's Expert Report makes no references to malingering in Mr. Ongwen, a key prong of Prof. W-P's and Dr. GM's critique, adopted by the Trial Chamber.

The Predicate Issue: Is a Critique of Methodology Racially and Culturally Biased or "Fair Game"?

It is my contention that the Trial Chamber's critique of methodology was implicitly biased against the Defence Experts, based on factors of culture and race. I am not saying that individual Judges on the *Ongwen* Bench were intentionally racist or intentionally culturally insensitive in their critique of the methodology of the Defence Experts. I am saying that these implicit or unconscious biases played a role in (a) how and on what basis the Chamber criticized the methodology, resulting in (b) its wholesale rejection of the content of the evidence as unreliable and, hence, not credible.

Critiques of methodology are routinely used by both the Prosecution and the Defence to undermine expert witnesses. One cannot categorically (and credibly) state that methodology can never be used to critique conclusions. It is illogical to argue against a premise which says that the means or process determines the results. If you view the two factors of process and results dialectically, it is obvious that they both impact on each other and on the content of the conclusions.

Methodology is not a neutral and impartial concept in psychiatry or in other disciplines. The choice and structure of methodology, and where/how/if it is applied, are related to context. In the case of forensic psychiatry, one has to ask: In what context is a particular methodology being applied? Does the methodology "work" based on the patient's cultural background? If no, can adjustments be made or does the methodology

---

[73] Raphael Lorenzo Aguiling Pangalangan, *Dominic Ongwen and the Rotten Social Background Defense: The Criminal Culpability of Child Soldiers Turned War Criminals*, 33(3) AM. UNIV. INT. LAW REV. (2018), Article 6, https://digitalcommons.wcl.american.edu/auilr/vol33/iss3/6.

have to be scrapped and replaced? What is the psychiatrist's cultural background, and does it affect the methodology? Does the methodology take cognizance of the cultural/racial identity of the patient, as well as the psychiatrist who is applying it? And, how do the answers to these questions inform the expected and actual results?

It is a fallacy that methodology in psychiatry is a cookie-cutter, one-size-fits-all concept. The methodology one chooses to use may be, by definition, biased and embody cultural and racial biases. These biases, which can be implicit or explicit (depending on who views them—the holder or the target of the biases), can become motivating factors in reaching a conclusion. And, without recognizing or accounting for these biases, the methodology critique itself becomes biased. This is what happened in the *Ongwen* case.

So, the short answer to the question "Is a critique of methodology 'fair game"? is "Yes." With a *caveat*: biases in methodology (especially when not acknowledged) nullify the legitimacy and fairness of using methodology as the basis of criticism.

Confirmation Bias and Biased Conclusions in the *Ongwen* Case

Linked to implicit and explicit biases is confirmation bias. Kassin et al., referencing studies over the last 40 years, define "confirmation bias" in the context of a criminal case:

> ...[W]e use the term forensic confirmation bias to summarize the class of effects through which an individual's preexisting beliefs, expectations, motives, and situational context influence the collection, perception, and interpretation of evidence during the course of a criminal case.[74]

[74] Saul M. Kassin, Itiel Dror and Jeff Kukucka, *The forensic confirmation bias: Problems, perspectives, and proposed solutions*, 2(1) J. APPL. RES. MEM. COGN. (2013), 42–52, 45, https://doi.org/10.1016/j.jarmac.2013.01.001. The Abstract reads (in part):

> ...In this article, we describe classic psychological research on primacy, expectancy effects, and observer effects, all of which indicate that context can taint people's perceptions, judgments, and behaviors. Then we describe recent studies indicating that confessions and other types of informa-

Generally, the concept of "confirmation bias" has been applied to beliefs about the guilt of a defendant, which could impact judicial decision-making. An example would be coerced confessions and other factors in the area of wrongful convictions.

Perhaps one of the most infamous examples in the United States of confirmation bias based on race is the case of Antron McCray, Kevin Richardson, Yusef Salaam, Raymond Santana, Jr. and Korey Wise ('The Central Park Five'). It is, however, only one of countless travesties of justice based on racism. On 19 April 1989, these five Black and Latino teenagers, between 14 and 16, were arrested in New York City's Central Park and charged with the assault and rape of a white jogger (Trisha Meili, known initially as the Central Park Jogger).[75] There was nothing to connect them to the crime: no physical evidence, no eyewitnesses. The coerced, false "confessions" were extracted under duress and torture by police. The young men were convicted and sentenced to terms of between five and fifteen years. In 2002, when Matias Reyes, a convicted rapist, confessed to the crime, the charges against The Central Park Five were vacated, and the young men were finally exonerated. They are now known as "The Exonerated Five." In 2014, New York City settled a federal civil-rights lawsuit with them for 41 million dollars.

From the first hours of the case, racism controlled most (white) media coverage and commandeered every step in the criminal justice system.[76] The Central Park Five case appears in Google as the first example for "confirmation bias in criminal justice."[77] It is the subject of the

tion can set into motion *forensic confirmation biases* that corrupt lay witness perceptions and memories as well as the judgments of experts in various domains of forensic science...." (italics in original)

[75] A sixth teenager, Steven Lopez, was also arrested in the case and pled guilty to robbery of a male jogger. He was exonerated in July 2022 when his conviction was vacated and the indictment dismissed.

[76] *See*, for example, Jelani Cobb, *The Central Park Five, Criminal Justice and Donald Trump*, THE NEW YORKER, Daily Comment, April 19, 2019 , The Central Park Five, Criminal Justice, and Donald Trump | The New Yorker. *Also see*, Central Park Five: Crime, Coverage & Settlement (history.com) (examples of racist coverage in media). There have been many articles, books, documentaries, and so on about the case.

[77] The Google entry states: One of the most notable examples of confirmation bias in the criminal justice system is the case of the Central Park Five. In 1989, five young black men were wrongfully convicted of raping a white woman in Central Park based on coerced confessions and a flawed investigation.

award-winning film "When They See Us," directed by Ava DuVernay, available on Netflix and other documentaries.

In *Ongwen*, the same concept of confirmation bias is applicable - whether to racial or cultural biases - based on the beliefs, motives and context which influence the Trial Chamber's interpretation of the evidence. But, to understand this, it is necessary to examine whether and how the confirmation bias of the individual Prosecution Experts, on whom the Chamber relied, impacted their evidence. The problem is not that Prof. W-P and Dr. GM had the objective to support the conclusion that Mr. Ongwen did not suffer from mental disease or defect. But, in the course of carrying this out, these Prosecution Experts failed to recognize their own biases, which rendered their evidence incredible and unreliable. I say this because it is inconceivable that any individual (a) would be "free from" confirmation bias, and (b) would not – spontaneously – have a tendency to seek out or interpret or recall information in a way that supports one's existing belief system. But professional experts in a Court should be held to higher standard, where they, at least, acknowledge their biases.

In the *Ongwen* case, the Trial Chamber's fundamental criticism of the Defence Experts' methodology was that it was deficient and outdated,[78] and therefore, yielded unreliable conclusions. This was based principally on the expert opinion of Prof. W-P, one of the three Prosecution experts, who was supported by Dr. GM.[79] This is illustrated, for example, by the Judgment's reliance on Prof. W-P's evidence, particularly in his Rebuttal Report.[80] The Chamber adopted the methodology critique of Prof. W-P and Dr. GM – which was laden with their pre-existing biased beliefs about race and culture and which influenced their professional judgment in *Ongwen.*

In the Judgment, Prof. W-P was treated as the "architect" of the Trial Chamber's methodology critique and rejection of the Defence Experts'

---

[78] Factors #2 and #5 in the Trial Chamber's list, *supra* are the context for this point. *See*, TJ: 2532–2535. *Also see*, TJ references to Rebuttal Case.

[79] DCB, para. 609 (n.996 Dr. Mezey Expert Report, UGA-OTP-0280-0786, paras. 43 and 81 [Defence Experts' reports criticized as "extremely credulous"]).

[80] TJ: 2496. *See*, TJ references to Rebuttal Report in Section on expert evidence of Prof. EO and Dr. DA at TJ: 2522 – 2574 referencing critique of Prof. W-P ("P-447") for each methodology factor.

evidence. But Prof. W-P's expert opinions were permeated with biases related to race and culture and these biases stretched his reliability and credibility very thin.[81] They not only tainted, but nullified his expert opinion on the Defence Experts' methodology. This problem was exacerbated because the Chamber embraced and relied on Prof. W-P's critique "lock, stock and barrel" - with no caution or *caveat.* It failed to dissociate itself from the tenor and content of Prof. W-P's critique, which embodied lack of professional respect for the Defence Experts. In so doing, the Chamber was also accepting the methodology critique *cum* racial and cultural biases of its architect as its own.

(1) Prof. Weierstall-Pust's contribution to judicial bias

(a) Prof. W-P'S critique of the Defence Experts' report as "sloppy"

In his Rebuttal Report, Prof. W-P characterized the Defence Experts' 2nd Report as "insufficient, or unfounded, or inconsistent, or contradictory or sloppy in every aspect and does not fulfil the minimal criteria of a professional forensic report according to current state-of-the art."[82] He also accused the Defence Experts of "degrading their [the ICC-DC][83] clinical ratings as sloppy clinical notes,"[84] but conceded on cross-examination that Dr. DA did not criticize the ICC-DC notes as sloppy.[85] Hence, Prof. W-P's false allegations simply evaporated under close scrutiny.

Finally, Prof. W-P admitted that although the Defence Experts and Prof. de Jong (a white European from the Netherlands) reached the same

---

[81] Credibility, including in a judicial setting, is not an abstract, absolute concept and it is not a neutral matter. Credibility determinations are based on "objective" and "subjective" criteria which are value-laden and affected by political, economic, cultural, racial, and other factors. This means that ICC judicial findings of credibility reflect the racial and cultural frame of reference of the "maker" of the findings, within the institutional framework of the ICC. *See* sections, *infra.* on cultural bias and scientific standards, and on language and culture in the CES-D test (determination of credibility of particular test is circumscribed by biases or prejudices in its content, as well as circumstances of test administration).

[82] DCB, para. 610.

[83] ICC-DC is the International Criminal Court's Detention Center in The Hague.

[84] DCB, para. 611.

[85] DCB, para. 612.

conclusions in respect to the mental illnesses from which Mr. Ongwen suffered, "sloppy" only applies to the Defence Experts and not to Prof. de Jong. Prof. W-P did not explain the disparate application.[86]

In response, the Defence Experts did not suggest that Prof. W-P had any racial *animus* toward them, but Prof. EO was clear that Prof. W-P's criticisms exceeded the parameters of professional criticism. In his rejoinder testimony, Prof. EO criticized Prof. W-P's characterizations of the Defence Experts' work as "deviant" and "sloppy." He noted that these descriptions did not reflect the standard of criticism within an academic, professional environment.[87]

As a Prosecution Expert, Prof. W-P's job was to critique the Defence Experts' evidence and reach the conclusion that it failed to support the affirmative defence of mental disease or defect. But, there is a big distinction between disagreeing with the outcomes or conclusions of a report and using words such as "sloppy" to trash its methodology. Words do matter—because the choice of words encapsulates prejudices and biases. I cannot help but wonder whether Prof. W-P would have chosen to characterize the Expert Report as "sloppy" if it had been presented by an expert who was white.

Unfortunately, the "sloppy" example cannot be "written off" as a single instance of a poor choice of words, or an error in language. This example exists within a context of repeated examples of bias.

(b) **Prof. W-P's "impression" of the Defence Experts' evidence on culture and mental illness**

Prof. W-P claimed that the Defence Experts' position was that a "non-African mental health professional could not be capable of diagnosing individuals from an African country."[88] There is no basis in the evidence for this statement, nor is there any evidence from which to make an inference. When pressed on cross-examination, Prof. W-P conceded it is his "impression during the court hearing …that contradictions were blamed

---

[86] DAJ, para. 372, n.424 (T-253, p. 31, l. 9 – p. 32, l. 21).

[87] *See*, DAJ, para. 372 for references.

[88] Prof. W-P's Rebuttal Report, p. 8; DAJ, para. 458. Both Prof. W-P and Dr. GM were non-Africans, with limited direct work on the African continent.

[for] a misunderstanding western psychiatrists have, who do not 'sense' the special conditions in the 'African context.'"[89]

So, what was the Defence Experts' evidence? They testified about the impact of culture on psychiatry[90] and the relation between symptoms and how they manifest, based on the culture of the patient.[91] Dr. Akena testified about the differences in respect to mental health in African and in Western societies. For example, he described the lack of mental health literacy in African populations, which meant that "most people in Africa cannot describe the signs and symptoms of depression by themselves." He testified that many African languages cannot translate the word "blues" so his patients do not say, "I am feeling blue...."[92]

This testimony is consistent with Prof. EO's evidence about the somatization and spiritualization of mental health problems in Africa. He explained that "[i]n our part of the world, we somatise. What that means is we convert psychological distress into physical symptoms. And we also spiritualise... we explain our psychological distress in the terms of the effects of the spirits, ancestral sprits, the wrong we have done. And the evils that our ancestors themselves did, we explain this, our distress, as punishment for events that other people in our lineage, if it wasn't us, performed or committed...."[93]

In their Rejoinder Rebuttal, the Defence Experts indicate that the work of Elialilia Sarikiaeli Okello[94] and Oye Gureje are "examples of individuals who have described explanatory models of mental illnesses in African populations."[95] The Defence Experts' point is that how, or even if, a patient perceives a mental illness and communicates this to a psychiatrist is bound by culture.

[89] DAJ, para. 457.

[90] DCB, para. 662.

[91] DCB, para. 663 and Dr. DA testimony on PTSD *infra* at n.164.

[92] DCB, para. 663, n.1073.

[93] T-254, p. 15, ll. 16–24.

[94] *See*, for example, Okello at n.165 *infra*.

[95] DAJ, paras. 456–458.

Thus, based on the evidence, Prof. W-P's "impression" is wrong.[96] Not only does he put words into the Defence Experts' mouths, but he turns their view into: non-African psychiatrists cannot diagnose mental illness in Africans in African societies. This was not their evidence. Prof. W-P's "interpretation" is, therefore, incorrect and misrepresents the record. But it also demonstrates that his implicit racial and cultural biases prevented him from comprehending the Defence Experts' evidence – in the courtroom and in Expert Reports – with any accuracy. Since the conclusions of Prof. W-P on methodology were not made on a sound, unabiased basis, they should not have been trusted and relied upon by the Trial Chamber.

(c) **Prof. W-P's DSM[97] critique and his "unclean hands"**

The Trial Judgment, based on Prof. W-P, found that the Defence Experts used an "outdated" system of classifications, that is, DSM-IV instead of DSM-5.[98] But this was false and not supported by the evidence; the Judgment had misrepresented the evidence.[99] The Defence Experts used the current DSM-5 for diagnostic criteria and used its predecessor, DSM-IV, solely for the format of the information in their report.[100] So, there should not have been any issue. But the Chamber's misstatement of the evidence is not the end of the story. It uncritically

[96] The Appeal Judgment bolsters and rehabilitates Prof. W-P's biases. Its argument is based on Prof. W-P's biased and subjective opinion that the Defence Experts were trying to deflect the criticisms of contradictions in their evidence by arguing that Western psychiatrists did not understand the African context. *See* AJ: 1321–22. In essence, the Appeals Chamber goes further than the Trial Judgment (starting at TJ: 2458) in its explanation and rehabilitation of Prof. W-P and his evidence.

[97] DSM is the DIAGNOSTIC AND STATISTICAL MANUAL OF MENTAL DISORDERS, published by the American Psychiatric Association. DSM-IV(Fourth Edition) was originally published in 1994, and a text-revised edition was published in 2000; DSM-5 (Fifth Edition) and its text-revised edition were both published in 2013.

[98] TJ: 2535.

[99] DAJ, paras. 345–350. The multi-axial system is a way to categorize disease and disorders, and factors which affect them. The system, used in DSM-IV, was not retained in DSM-5 based on criticisms from clinicians. DSM-5 adopted a "non-axial" approach but retained the categories and content of the old axes in DSM-IV. This is explained in DSM-5, section on "The Multiaxial System" at p. 16. But, the bottom line is that diagnostic criteria were not changed from DSM-IV to DSM-5.

[100] DCB. Paras. 651–653; DAJ, paras. 342–350.

relied on Prof. W-P, although he did not have "clean hands" in the DSM "controversy."[101] In fact, he had been involved in a study in which the choice of DSM edition was addressed.

Prof. W-P was one of the co-authors of a research study in which the outdated DSM-IV was used, although the updated DSM-5 was in effect during the second data collection, and arguably for most of the first data collection, and at the time the study was submitted for publication. The article was entitled, "The cycle of violence as a function of PTSD and appetitive aggression: A longitudinal study with Burundian soldiers"[102] ("Burundi Study"). It was received by Wiley's journal, *Aggressive Behavior*, 27 August 2019 and first published in May 2020, and then in September/October 2020, Vol. 46, Issue 5 at pp. 391–399. About three months after the article was submitted, Prof. W-P testified and submitted his Rebuttal Report in the *Ongwen* Rebuttal Case, on 25–26 November 2019. The Burundi Study was being considered for publication at the time of the *Ongwen* Rebuttal Case.

The crux of the problem is that the Burundi Study, at Section 2.3.1, states that "DSM-IV was chosen as DSM-5 had not been validated at the time of the first data collection." This is not entirely true: The American Psychiatric Association (APA) Board of Trustees approved the recommendation for DSM-5 about a month into the first data collection. The second data collection was conducted after DSM-5 had been published.

- **November 2012** – The APA Assembly recommended that the DSM-5 (published in 2013) be approved by the APA Board of Trustees;
- **November 2012–January 2013** – First data collection in Burundi Study of 488 male Burundian soldiers. The start was simultaneous to the APA's Assembly approval;
- **December 2012** – APA Board of Trustees approved Assembly's recommendation;
- **2013** – DSM-5 published;

[101] *See, Prosecutor v. Ongwen*, ICC-02/04-01/15, Defence Response to the *Amici Curiae* Observations, Document 1950 (January17, 2022), para. 52, n.96.

[102] Corina Nandi, Anselm Crombach, Thomas Elbert, Manassé Bambonye, Rüdiger Pryss, Johannes Schobel, Roland Weierstall-Pust, The cycle of violence as a function of PTSD and appetitive aggression: A longitudinal study with Burundian soldiers (wiley.com)

- **March–July 2014** – Second data collection in Burundi Study of 468 soldiers.

Experts can differ about which DSM edition is applicable, and theoretically, one can argue that the period of the collection of the first data was a "grey area" as to which DSM edition applied.

But I am not using this example to make a determination about which DSM edition applies in the Burundi Study. I am using it to highlight the failure of Prof. W-P to disclose his own involvement, as a co-author in a research study in which the choice of DSM was an issue addressed in the study.

In *Ongwen*, Prof. W-P's testimony criticizing the Defence Experts for using an "outdated" DSM edition was a significant argument in the Trial Chamber's rejection of their evidence.[103] Had this information about the Burundi Study been disclosed by Prof. W-P to the Court, it would have provided reasonable doubt as to the reliability and credibility of Prof. W-P's criticism,[104] especially in his Rebuttal Report. Prof W-P's "lapse" in judgment in respect to disclosure rendered his evidence on methodology, particularly related to usage of an "outdated" DSM edition, unreliable.

Lastly, it is important to note that the Court-Appointed Expert, Prof. de Jong, in an interview, specifically criticized one of the Prosecution Experts (referring to Prof. W-P, who was not named in the interview) for his professional opinions in *Ongwen*, including his testimony that people in combat cannot suffer from PTSD. Yet, this was opposite to the conclusion the Prosecution Expert had reached in the Burundi Study, in which he was a co-author.[105] In *Ongwen*, Prof. W-P's evidence was that a)

[103] TJ: 2533–2534.

[104] In addition, Prof. W-P's representation of the DSM-5 is not accurate: in his Rebuttal Report, UGA-OTP-0287-0072, p. 0078, he states that in the Defence Experts' Second Psychiatric Report (SPR), "multi-axial diagnosis is part of outdated DSM-IV." First, the "multi-axial format" in SPR is used for format, not content (all diagnoses are based on DSM-5 diagnostic criteria – *see*, SPR at -0971). Second, the DSM-5's Introduction, Section 1, p. 16, states that the revision in DSM-5 is consistent with text in DSM-IV.

[105] *See*, Marina Fortuna, *The Psychological Assessment of the Defendant in the Ongwen case: An interview with Prof. Joop de Jong*, GROJIL, 8 September 2021. This is a summary of an interview which the author conducted with Prof. de Jong. In it, she mistakenly refers to a Court-Appointed Expert, when – in fact – the reference should be to a Prosecution Expert (who is Prof. Weierstall-Pust ["P-447"]), on whom the Court relied, particularly his Rebuttal evidence, for its conclusions in the Trial Judgment. *See*, TJ: 2532–2535.

someone with PTSD would not be able to use a weapon, be promoted, become an administrator; in other words, PTSD rendered the person dysfunctional (in contrast to Mr. Ongwen). In the same interview, Prof. de Jong also criticized the Expert's argument that Mr. Ongwen was not depressed because he works hard and pays attention to his children. Prof. de Jong characterized this as "another display of professional naïveté." Prof. de Jong cautioned: "...If the [P]rosecution gets away with this kind of biased and flawed opinions, the ICC runs the risk that serious experts in the future may turn their backs on the tribunal..."[106]

The 180 Degree Turnaround: Expert Evidence of Professor Weierstall-Pust and Dr. Mezey in *Al Hassan* Case[107]

Two of the Prosecution Experts in *Ongwen*, Dr. GM and Prof. W-P, were also appointed (in August 2020, about six months after Closing Arguments in *Ongwen*) by the *Al Hassan* Trial Chamber X to conduct a Rule 135 examination of Mr. Al Hassan to assess his competency to stand trial. Together with a third expert in torture, they constituted a Panel of Experts ("POE").[108]

What is striking about the *Al Hassan* Report[109] is that the two former *Ongwen* Prosecution Experts made a 180-degree "about face" in the *Al Hassan* case on the same issues about which they gave expert evidence in *Ongwen*—methodology, impact of cultural factors on mental health,[110]

---

[106] *Ibid.*, Fortuna interview with Prof. de Jong.

[107] *See*, Defence Response to the *Amici Curiae* Observations, 17 January 2022, Doc 1950, paras. 51–52.

[108] *Al Hassan* Decision, paras. 9 and 32. The third expert was Dr. Korzinski, who was supported by the Trial Chamber X (a different Trial Chamber than in *Ongwen*) and the Registry because of his expertise in developing culturally sensitive methods in assessing complex trauma.

[109] Report on the Medical Examination, pursuant to Rule 135 of the Rules of Procedure and Evidence of Mr. Al Hassan ("*Al Hassan* Report"), ICC-01/12-018-1197-Anx-Red-23-03-2021, Summary of POE's opinion and recommendations, p. 46, paras. 321–328.

[110] *See*, *Al Hassan* Report, especially noting Prof. W-P, who concluded that Mr. Al Hassan had a complex trauma-disorder taking into account cultural and biographical (individual) background. In the same Report, Dr. GM found no sign of mental disorder, p. 4.

use of the DSM standards, and malingering. Comparing their *modus operandi* in *Ongwen* with their Rule 135 Report in *Al Hassan*, it is as if they were totally different Experts. While mental health assessments are individual, and made on a case-by-case basis, the marked difference in the Experts' attitude and approach in each case is inescapable. For example, in the *Al Hassan* case, Prof. W-P and Dr. GM displayed a collegial attitude toward Defence Experts with whom they disagreed; this was opposite to their virulent criticisms of the *Ongwen* Defence Experts.[111]

Because the Prosecution Experts' evidence was relied upon by the *Ongwen* Trial Chamber to reject the Article 31(1)(a) defence, it is even more important to compare their professional approaches in each case. Their inconsistent and opposite approaches diminish their professional integrity and militate against the Chamber's reliance on them for their methodology critique.

The question is: Did the Trial Chamber in *Ongwen* take this stark inconsistency in approach into account, before it adopted its methodology critique, based on Prof. W-P and Dr. GM? And if yes, why does the Chamber fail to address the inconsistency? Or, did it simply choose to ignore the discrepancies?

The *Al Hassan* Report was dated 8 December 2020, about two months prior to the *Ongwen* Trial Judgment on 4 February 2021. The *Ongwen* Prosecution had a duty to disclose this information under the Rome Statute, Article 67(2) because it "may affect the credibility of prosecution evidence." The Prosecution did not disclose the report to the Defence until after the *Ongwen* Trial Judgment. However, it also had a duty when the *Al Hassan* Report was received to disclose it to the Trial Chamber IX – which was deliberating on the *Ongwen* case. The *Al Hassan* Report was extremely relevant to the assessment of evidence of the two Prosecution Experts, Prof. W-P and Dr. GM, who also testified in *Ongwen*.[112]

---

[111] *See, infra* contrasting Prof. W-P's and Dr. GM's attitudes in *Ongwen* and *Al Hassan*'s cases.

[112] I do not know if the *Al Hassan* Report was disclosed in a timely manner to the *Ongwen* Chamber. The Defence received the Report from the Prosecution on 23 March 2021, the same day that it filed a public redacted version with the Registry. But, the *Ongwen* Trial Chamber should have considered the Prosecutions Experts' inconsistencies within the *Al Hassan* Report with their evidence in the *Ongwen* case—on identical issues in both cases: approach to culture and mental illness, malingering and self-reporting, methodology and Defence Experts' evidence.

(1) **Comparison of the positions of Dr. GM and Prof. W-P in *Ongwen* and *Al Hassan***

(a) **On methodology and treatment of other Experts:** In *Al Hassan,* there is a marked difference from *Ongwen* in the attitude of the POE[113] toward the Defence Experts involved in the case. In *Al Hassan*, the *Ongwen* Prosecution Experts, Dr. GM and Prof. W-P, displayed a collegial and professional attitude toward other Experts involved in the case.[114] First, they did not attack or try to discredit the *Al Hassan* Defence Experts' methodology as they had done in *Ongwen.*[115]

Second, the *Ongwen* Prosecution Experts acknowledged when their findings were also consistent with reports and notes of other Experts in *Al Hassan.*[116] Even though Prof. W-P and Dr. GM disagreed with the three *Al Hassan* Defence Experts on a number of issues,[117] it is clear that they valued and relied on the Defence Experts' reports for information about the allegations of torture, a key factor in the POE's conclusions and recommendations—especially because the POE was "not permitted to assess the specific incidents that happened to AH [Mr. Al Hassan] during the period of alleged torture" in Mali.[118]

Third, the POE used respectful and professional language in describing disagreements with Defence Experts as "differing views of his [Mr. Al Hassan] status as a victim and issue of alleged torture."[119] "Differing views" is a far cry from "outdated" "unscientific" and "sloppy" found in Prof. W-P's evidence. In *Ongwen*,

---

[113] The *Al Hassan* Report was prepared by the POE. Prof. W-P is referred to as "RWP" in the *Al Hassan* Report. For consistency, I continue to use Prof. W-P in this section.

[114] *Al Hassan* Report, paras. 4, 230 and 288.

[115] TJ: 2528–2574. *See*, DAJ, paras. 323–419 and DCB, paras. 604–674.

[116] *Al Hassan* Report, para. 235 (AH has symptoms which would represent a manifestation of PTSD).

[117] One issue was whether Mr. Al Hassan was a victim based on allegations of torture, or whether he was also an alleged perpetrator (discussed in Report, para. 230).

[118] *Al Hassan* Report, para. 171 ("evaluation of the exposure to torture could only be reconstructed from files made available to the POE, in particular.....reports of Crosby, Cohen and Porterfield [Defence Experts]")

[119] *Al Hassan* Report, para. 230.

there was no recognition of the Defence Experts' decades of professional experience and expertise, both in academia and in practice, at national and international levels.

Fourth, in *Al Hassan*, Prof. W-P and Dr. GM endorsed the practice of open-ended questions for victims of torture.[120] But, in *Ongwen*, Prof. W-P's position on open-ended questions was the opposite: the Trial Judgment relied on his methodology critique (in his Rebuttal Report) of open-ended questions to disregard and discredit the evidence of the Defence Experts.[121]

(b) **On the DSM "gold standard"**: The salient point in the *Al Hassan* Report is that the DSM is not treated as the one and only way to analyze mental health and factors which impact on it. Yet, in *Ongwen*, the DSM was the treated in the Judgment as the one and only standard – period. In the *Al Hassan* Report, the POE articulated a flexibility, or lack of dogmatism and rigidity in using the DSM categories to characterize Mr. Al Hassan's situation. The title of one of the Report's sections says it all: Cultural Considerations and Limitations surrounding the diagnosis of PTSD. Here, the POE criticizes the limitations of a "purely categorical approach" in the DSM which does not take account of individual circumstances or cultural and religious differences as they apply to disorders and symptoms of distress. They posit that in assessing PTSD there is a danger that categories can be applied to limit its existence, at the risk of implying that no torture was experienced. As a result, the importance and validity of disorders or signs of distress that may not meet DSM thresholds are simply discounted.[122]

(c) **On standardized testing**: In *Al Hassan*, Dr. GM and Prof. W-P demonstrated a flexibility toward using standardized testing based

[120] *Al Hassan* Report, para. 202.

[121] TJ: 2532–2535.

[122] *Al Hassan* Report, para. 203 ("there are recognized limitations in using a purely categorical approach [e.g. failure to capture individual, cultural and religious differences in disorder severity, and clinically significant features subsumed by other disorders or idioms of distress falling below outside conventional DMS thresholds])."

on the specific circumstances and culture of the defendant.[123] This was accompanied by a view that mental health conditions can change.[124] Yet, in *Ongwen*, the Trial Chamber, relying on Prof. W-P's critique of the Defence Experts' methodology, used their failure to assess malingering with a psychometric test as one of the key reasons for the unreliability of their evidence.[125]

(d) **On self-reporting and malingering:** Both Mr. Al Hassan and Mr. Ongwen provided information on their respective mental health through self-reporting. In *Ongwen*, Prof. W-P and Dr. GM were unequivocal that Mr. Ongwen was malingering, in order to discredit his self-reporting. The Trial Chamber agreed, concluding that nothing that Mr. Ongwen self-reported could be taken as true. The *Ongwen* Defence Experts' acceptance of self-reporting and failure to diagnose malingering was a key element in the Chamber's methodology critique and rejection of their evidence.[126]

In *Al Hassan*, the POE's conclusions about malingering were the opposite of the Prosecution Experts' in *Ongwen*: the Report states that Mr. Al Hassan "did not appear to be prone to exaggeration or distress or fabrication of symptoms...he did not use these opportunities for feigning distress or malingering."[127] This was preceded by 30 paragraphs of Mr. Al Hassan's self-reporting on family and personal history of mental disorders, culturally rooted sense of

---

[123] *Al Hassan* Report, para. 203 ("there are recognized limitations in a purely categorical approach...the complexity of the human condition does not slot itself neatly into diagnostic categories..."). *See also*, Alfredo Ardila, *Cultural Values Underlying Psychometric Cognitive Testing*, 15(4) NEUROPSYCHOL. REV. 185–95, 192 (Dec 2005), DOI: https://doi.org/10.1007/s11065-005-9180-y (psychometric cognitive testing is only appropriate in those societies with a solid psychometric tradition, basically, Western societies); Neil Krishan Aggarwal, *Culture, Communication, and DSM-5 Diagnostic Reliability*, 109(3) J. NATL. MED. ASSOC. 149-220 at 150-152 (Autumn 2017), DOI: https://doi.org/10.1016/j.jnma.2017.03.005 (discussing the role of cultural and racial factors in making diagnoses, and the need for DSM-5 field studies to address actual experiences of care of different populations who are part of the field studies).

[124] *Al Hassan* Report, para. 238 ("Fitness [to stand trial] is not a static state but is a dynamic variable which may change according to circumstances...").

[125] TJ: 2532–35. *See*, DAJ, paras. 343–353; DCB, paras. 651–653.

[126] TJ: 2558–68. *See* DAJ, paras. 393–409 and DCB, paras. 667–673.

[127] *Al Hassan* Report, para. 129.

betrayal and degradation, prior understanding and experience with international law and with mental health professionals.[128]

In respect to the torture allegations, not only did the POE rely on information from the Defence Experts, but they clearly considered Mr. Al Hassan's self-reporting and gave him the benefit of the doubt. Mr. Al Hassan provided accounts of his torture in Mali and alleged that the OTP was complicit in this torture. The POE states: "*We have no reason not to believe Mr. Al Hassan's account of this*, which has been fairly consistent over time…."[129] (italics added)

In addition, the POE factored in Mr. Al Hassan's self-report in their assessment and recommendations. Mr. Al Hassan self-reported that he had no mental health problems before the torture and that his arrest and torture changed this. Based on this, the POE assessed all trauma-related questions in relation to trauma triggers that stem from torture or interrogation experiences.[130]

Moreover, the POE concludes that although Mr. Al Hassan has no current impairment to the exercise of his fair trial rights, his belief that the case against him is built on evidence extracted under torture [in Mali] could compromise these rights.[131] They also conclude that his experiences with torture could impact on his right to testify. If this were to occur, "the defence would be truly disadvantaged."[132]

In sum, the POE emphasized the serious potential of the torture allegations to impact on Mr. Al Hassan's fair trial rights, even though it was not permitted to independently investigate or access information about the torture allegations and was not provided with any information about these allegations by the Trial Chamber.[133]

[128] *Ibid.*, paras. 66–96.

[129] *Ibid.*, paras. 301–302.

[130] *Ibid.*, para. 173.

[131] *Ibid.*, paras. 292–294.

[132] *Ibid.*, paras. 282–283 (Mr. Al Hassan's experience would constitute a condition that may impact on his ability to give testimony and withstand cross-examination)

[133] *Al Hassan* Report, paras. 62, 171.

(e) **On culture and religion**: The importance of culture and religion in addressing the mental health issues in *Al Hassan* was fully integrated into Prof. W-P's and Dr. GM's analysis and suggestions. For example, there is a lengthy discussion of the role of religion in coping strategies, and an explicit effort to co-ordinate Islamic beliefs with Western psychology.[134] Their sensitivity to culture in *Al Hassan* is in contrast to *Ongwen,* where the two Prosecution Experts dismissed cultural factors.[135]

(f) **On culture and mental illness:** In *Al Hassan*, the POE considered the cultural context in their diagnosis of PTSD, and integrated cultural factors into their analysis. They concluded that Mr. Al Hassan was fit to plead, and not currently (at the time he was examined) suffering from PTSD or any other recognized psychiatric disorder.[136] However, they did not completely rule out PTSD. Mr. Al Hassan could have previously suffered from PTSD or could be at risk in the future for late-onset PTSD.[137] Their Report recommended a "trauma-informed approach"[138] and that cultural and religious factors, including co-operation with Mr. Al Hassan's Imam, was necessary to ensure Mr. Al Hassan's mental health status.[139] If this was not done, then Mr. Al Hassan might be unable to exercise his fair trial rights, including

[134] *Al Hassan* Report, paras. 305–312. *See also* paras. 285–286 (Mr. Al Hassan is fit to plead according to narrow criteria [discussed previously], but cultural and other variables must also be considered as criteria in applying this in a modern judicial system).

[135] DAB, paras. 451–458.

[136] *Al Hassa*n Report, Summary of Opinion and Recommendations, paras. 321–328.

[137] *Ibid.*, para. 206. *See also,* para. 235 (differences between Prof. W-P and MK, the third expert, with Dr. GM on whether post-traumatic symptoms are a manifestation of PTSD).

[138] *Al Hassan* Report, para. 297.

[139] The POE recommended that "Western mental health options should be coordinated with his Iman as to ensure both approaches are congruent and complementary with one another" (para. 313). *See also,* paras. 306–312.

the right to give testimony if he chose to do so.[140] Generally, the POE did not display a rigid approach to indices of trauma.[141]

But in *Ongwen*, Prof. W-P and Dr. GM did not factor in Mr. Ongwen's cultural or religious context when they concluded that he was not suffering from PTSD. Hence, the Prosecution Experts' approach to PTSD illustrates the impact of cultural bias on their diagnoses in the *Ongwen* case.

(g) **On historic individual circumstances and mental health:** The view of Prof. W-P and Dr. GM in *Al Hassan* that individual circumstances count in mental health assessments contrasts with their position in *Ongwen*. In *Al Hassan*, Dr. GM and Prof. W-P recognized the long-term effects of PTSD as well as the impact of adverse childhood experiences on trauma.[142] In *Ongwen*, both ruled out PTSD in the case of Mr. Ongwen.[143] The Trial Chamber denied the relevance of Mr. Ongwen's abduction as a child and rejected its negative, lasting effects on Mr. Ongwen.[144]

(2) PTSD and cultural bias in the *Ongwen* case

That Mr. Ongwen was suffering from PTSD should have been a "no brainer"—but somehow, the Prosecution Experts and the Judgment missed this. The Defence Experts and the Court-Appointed Expert, Prof.

---

[140] *Al Hassan* Report, paras. 290–291 (highlighting burden and risk of participation in a trial and interference of trauma in exercise of fair trial rights, based on a wider interpretation of trauma criteria)

[141] Importantly, the findings in *Al Hassan* on PTSD are under Section 7.2.3 "Cultural Considerations and Limitations of the *Al Hassan* Report surrounding the Diagnosis of PTSD" at p. 29. At para. 206, Dr. GM and Prof. W-P did not concur about the implications of late onset PTSD, but the Report is careful to recognize that Mr. Al Hassan may have suffered from PTSD in the past or is at risk for future PTSD.

[142] *Al Hassan* Report, paras. 69–70 and 206 (Report recognizes that Mr. Al Hassan may have suffered from PTSD in the past or is at risk for future PTSD).

[143] *Al Hassan* Report, paras. 203, 289, 290 and 321–324. Compare to Mezey Report, UGA-OTP-0280-0786, paras. 62 and 89–92 and Prof. W-P Report, UGA-OTP-0280-0674, pp 16, 18 and 27–28. *See*, DCB, paras. 586–591.

[144] TJ: 2592. *See*, DAJ, para. 614, n.751.

de Jong, concurred that Mr. Ongwen suffered from PTSD, and his continuing trauma stemmed from his abduction as a child soldier in the LRA. Prof. de Jong characterized the PTSD as severe and suggested that "complex PTSD" may "best capture" Mr. Ongwen's trauma experiences.[145]

The Defence Experts also noted the similar manifestations of PTSD and of *cen* and *orongo*. A paper, by Prof. EO, one of the Defence Experts and Dr. Abbo, one of the Prosecution Experts, entitled "'*Orongo*' and '*Cen*' Spirit Possession—Post-Traumatic Stress Disorder in a Cultural Context: Local Problem, Universal Disorder with Local Solutions in Northern Uganda"[146] was entered into evidence by the Defence.

The main point of the paper is that when dealing with a universal psychiatric concept, it is necessary to look at its specific cultural expressions and resolutions. It starts with the premise that PTSD is "a universal condition that has affected humans for ages."[147] The authors point out that PTSD is a relatively new diagnosis dating back to 1980 when it appeared in the American diagnostic system, yet a concept of PTSD has existed in traditional Acholi illness concepts in Northern Uganda "for ages before the arrival of modern psychiatric practice."[148] In Northern Uganda, PTSD has been associated with the life-threatening experience of hunting and with inter-communal wars. It affects not only the individual but also the person's family and community. Within this framework, the article discusses "*orongo*" (animal) spirit possession and "*cen*" spirit possession and the Acholi cleansing rituals to prevent mental illness and promote peace between humans and the spirits or dead animals or human victims of killing. This includes the *Mato Oput* ceremony and the significance of ritual shrines (*Kac* and *Abila*).

---

[145] *See*, DCB, paras. 536–540.

[146] Emilio Ovuga and Catherine Abbo, *"Orongo" and "Cen" Spirit Possessions: Post-Traumatic Stress Disorder in a Cultural Context – Local Problem, Universal Disorder with Local Solutions in Northern Uganda*. In: Martin, C., Preedy, V. and Patel, V. (eds), COMPREHENSIVE GUIDE TO POST-TRAUMATIC STRESS DISORDERS, Springer, Cham (2015), https://doi.org/10.1007/978-3-319-08359-9_89. *See*, DCB, para. 666.

[147] Ovuga and Abbo, p. 1.

[148] Ovuga and Abbo, p. 1.

Both Prof. W-P and Dr. GM rejected that Mr. Ongwen suffered from PTSD, but the approach of Prof. W-P was slightly more open to the idea that he had suffered trauma, although the trauma did not rise to level of PTSD. Neither considered the cultural aspects of PTSD, and Dr. GM, in fact, admitted that she had not read the article by Prof. Ovuga and Dr. Abbo.[149]

The Trial Chamber, based mostly on evidence from Prof. W-P and Dr. GM, found that Mr. Ongwen was not suffering from PTSD or any other mental disease.[150] Although the Chamber had been presented with conflicting evidence from the Defence Experts, it refused to apply the reasonable doubt standard, that is, the Prosecution had to disprove beyond a reasonable doubt that Mr. Ongwen was not suffering from PTSD.

The Trial Chamber latched onto Prof. W-P's argument that Mr. Ongwen's "functionality" contradicted having PTSD (or any mental illness).[151] PTSD, a well-publicized mental illness, can affect individuals who are also functional members of society.[152] In addition, one of the *Ongwen* Victims' Experts, Prof. Wessels, gave evidence that child soldiers show resiliency when confronted with the worst imaginable situations.[153] Prof. EO explained that child soldiers mask their true feelings, especially in the LRA, which penalized young abductees for "showing feelings." He (and Prof. de Jong) also discussed reaction formation—the exhibiting of emotion or expressions which are contradictory to what one feels inside.[154] All together—these add up to the conclusion that a person suffering from PTSD (or other mental illness) can also find a way to be functional in her or his particular setting.

---

[149] T-163, p. 26, ll. 20–25 – p. 27, ll. 1–4.

[150] TJ: 2580. In respect to PTSD, the Prosecution Experts were not unanimous. *See*, DCB, paras. 659–660.

[151] TJ: 2493–2496.

[152] It is important to note, as Tze-Ern Chua points out, that mental illness is in the "limelight" when a famous person is suffering from it, but "when mental illness happens to ordinary people on an everyday basis, however, it can go unnoticed." Tze-Ern Chua, *Mental Illness, The Big Blind Spot*, Editorial, 2(2) J. OF CLIN. PSYCHIATRY (2016), Mental Illness: The Big Blind Spot (primescholars.com).

[153] DCB, para. 644; DAJ, para. 363.

[154] DCB, paras. 626–627.

Culture, Mental Health and Implicit Bias

That culture impacts on mental health should not be controversial. This has been officially recognized in the DSM-5,[155] International Classification of Diseases (ICD-11)[156] as well as within the medical literature.

As Laurence J. Kirmayer stated two decades ago: "Even though mental disorders can be found in every culture globally, the lived experience, expression of associated distress, and interpretation as evidence of deviance from acceptable norms are influenced by social cultural context."[157]

In the *Ongwen* case, Prof. EO and Dr. DA (as well as the Court-Appointed Expert, Prof. de Jong in a post-trial interview) supported that culture matters in mental health.[158] Even Prof. W-P acknowledged in his Rebuttal Report that Dr. DA was correct to highlight the "general necessity" to view and interpret a patient's symptoms within her/his cultural context.[159] But, the Trial Chamber failed to heed Prof. W-P's opinion on this topic. Instead, cultural bias affected its Judgment.

---

[155] In DSM-5, Cultural Concepts of Distress are discussed (pp. 758–759), and the criterion of "Culture-Related Diagnostic Issues" is applied to specific disorders. The DSM-5 identifies why cultural concepts are important to psychiatric diagnoses, including to avoid misdiagnosis, to obtain useful clinical information, to improve clinical rapport and engagement, to improve therapeutic efficacy, to guide clinical research and to clarify the cultural epidemiology. Cultural concepts have been a source of contention as well in the profession: *See*, n.123, *supra* on Aggarwal's critique of DSM-5 field trials and importance of a remedy to factor in race and ethnicity of both patient and clinician in collection and analysis of field data.

There are numerous publications on culture and mental illness; *see*, for example, Dinesh Bhugra, Cameron Watson and Rajiv Wijesuriya, *Editorial on Culture and mental illnesses*, 33(1–2, 1–2) INT. REV.OF PSYCHIATRY (2021), Full article: Culture and mental illnesses (tandfonline.com) (concludes that "cultural beliefs and values represent a crucial factor in mental illness").

[156] *See*, Oye Gureje, Roberto Lewis-Fernandez, Brian J. Hall and Geoffrey M. Reed, *Cultural Considerations in the Classification of Mental Disorders: Why and how in ICD-11*, BMC MED. 18, 25 (2020), https://doi.org/10.1186/s12916-020-1493-4 (importance of ICD-11 in providing guidance on culture issues to inform clinicians' decision-making).

[157] L. J. Kirmayer, *Cultural variations in the clinical presentation of depression and anxiety: Implications for diagnosis and treatment*, 62 J. OF CLIN. PSYCHIATRY (2001) 22–30. Quoted in Akin Ojagbemi and Oye Gureje, *Sociocultural contexts of mental illness experience among Africans*, 58(4) TRANSCULT. PSYCHIATRY (2021), 455–459.

[158] *See*, DCB, paras. 607–608, 662–666; DAJ, paras. 430–470 (Grounds 30, 34, 36 and 43 – Trial Chamber's errors related to culture and mental health issues, and assessment of Prosecution's Experts on culture). *See also* Fortuna, Interview with Prof. de Jong (difficult to divorce culture from psychology), *supra* at n.105.

[159] DCB, para. 655 for other references.

(1) The Trial Chamber's cultural stance: oblivion or conscious indifference?

The core of the Trial Chamber's cultural bias was demonstrated by its failure to appreciate the interplay of the universality of symptoms with the specifics of the cultural context. The position of the Defence Experts was that the universality of symptoms and specific cultural context impacted on each other. And, in respect to their own cultural identities, Prof. EO explained that holding a cultural belief system similar to a patient is helpful in understanding the patient, "but it does not affect the way we make our conclusions [...]."[160] The Defence Experts' similar cultural roots obviously place them in a position to better hear and listen to Mr. Ongwen and understand the political, social and cultural contexts in which he was forced to survive in the LRA. But their psychiatric conclusions were based on recognized diagnostic criteria within the profession, as applied to a particular cultural environment.[161]

Yet, the Trial Chamber could not or did not hear the Defence Experts' position that while there may be universal or core symptoms for a psychiatric illness, the expression of these symptoms and how they are perceived is determined by the cultural context.

As Prof. EO testified, "culture and psychiatry cannot be separated during this modern practice."[162] Dr. DA was asked by the Defence whether the core symptoms of PTSD manifest themselves more or less similarly across cultures. Dr. DA responded that the manifestation of mental illnesses would be similar across cultures, but the diagnosis relies on other factors which are determined by the cultural context:

---

[160] DCB, para. 607.

[161] The Trial Judgment did not explicitly criticize the Defence Experts for who they were—Ugandan psychiatrists—or where they worked and lived during the same period as the crimes charged in the UPDF war against the LRA. Instead, it chose to attack their "objectivity" by criticizing them for blurring the line between "treating" and "forensic" psychiatrist, thus destroying any "objectivity" (Methodological Factor #1). The Trial Chamber (and Prosecution, which was the source of this labeling) did not refer to any evidence to support their contention. *See*, TJ: 2528–2531; DAJ, paras. 329–341.

[162] DCB, para. 607.

> ...the core symptoms [of PTSD], yes, would be similar across cultures, but the diagnosis of mental illness doesn't rely squarely on the core symptoms....[it] rel[ies] on a number of things. And that's why when we are reporting, when you read text, when you read literature everywhere you come across things like the prevalence of PTSD or depression, varies or is—they usually give a range....of maybe 5 to 7 per cent, and then even the world mental health surveys, they will tell you, maybe in Africa this is the prevalence, in East Asia it's this, in Western Europe, it's that, in the US—so how do we come up with those variations? We come up with those variations because of these kinds of differences. We come up with those variations because even when you administer the same instruments in English, [in] the US, and then you administer the same instrument in Uganda to somebody who speaks English, for example, chances are that you may not get the same responses, you may not get the same way they understand this. And these are the things that affect the prevalences....So whereas patients would all complain [about] or present with in the case of post-traumatic stress disorder, they would have been exposed, they are avoiding situations, they are hypervigilant, etc., etc. The way in which each of those symptoms manifests may vary based on [one] where somebody comes from, and two, how they understand the question that they have been asked, whether it makes sense to them or not. Some questions.... are difficult to assess. I'll give an example. There's a famous screening instrument for depression called CES-D [CES-D is Center for Epidemiologic Studies Depression Scale] which is used for screening depression in general populations. I think question number 3 of the CES-D asks something like have you been feeling blue, [it] talks about blues.[163] Many African languages cannot translate the word "blues," so if you ask somebody that question in Africa and.... and some other places, they don't understand what that means. So how do you ask that question in our setting? That's just one of

[163] Question 3 on the CES-D reads: I felt that I could not shake off the blues. *See* Figure 1 in Jung Jae Lee, Ki Woong Kim, Tae Hui Kim, Joon Hyuk Park, Seok Bum Lee, Jin Woo Park, Douglas R. McQuoid, David C. Steffens, *Cross-cultural considerations in administering the center for epidemiologic studies depression scale*, 57(5) GERONTOLOGY. 2011, 455–461, doi: 10.1159/000318030. Lee et al. compared the diagnostic accuracy of the Center for Epidemiologic Studies Depression Scale (CES-D) for major depressive disorder (MDD) in late life between Korean and US Caucasian elderly. *They concluded that cross-cultural issues significantly influenced the diagnostic accuracy of depression questionnaires. Questionnaires developed in the Western culture should be culturally adapted and well translated linguistically to ensure comparability between ethnic groups.* (italics added).

> the examples of how context matters. If you talk about feeling blue in Western Europe, in the US, everybody understands what you mean. If you talk about feeling blue in Africa, people don't understand what you're saying. They don't know what blues means.... So it is those little differences that make these variations that we see happen."[164]

Elialilia Sarikiaeli Okello[165] posits that while the "dysphoric mood may be a universal human phenomenon, the concept of depressive disorder which focuses on mood change as a primary or core factor has evolved within a Western culture and may not be universally applicable."[166] She describes how the *Baganda* in Uganda conceptualize and treat depression as a clan illness, with its collective group origin in a faulty relationship between the living and the dead; this requires a collective healing process which involves the healer, patient and clan members.[167] Its roots and remedies are found outside of Western medicine.

However, the diagnostic labeling of depression reflects how depression is perceived in Western culture:

> ...the major issue in the classification of depression is that the diagnostic label is derived from Western language where the term depression is seen as being closely linked to mood change....[168]

Thus, culture impacts on all components of mental illness: its conception and perception, and diagnosis and labeling within the profession.

---

[164] Dr. DA Testimony, ICC-02/04-01/15-T-248, p. 46, ll. 1–25 – p. 47, ll. 1–22.

[165] *See,* Elialilia Sarikiaeli Okello, CULTURAL EXPLANATORY MODELS OF DEPRESSION IN UGANDA, Karolinska University Press, Stockholm, 2006, http://www.dspace.mak.ac.ug/bitstream/handle/10570/2029/okello-elialilia-sarikiaeli-chs-medicine-phd.pdf?sequence=1&isAllowed=y. Dr. Okello's research—between March 2003 and March 2005—is based on data collected during the "charged period" which the Trial Chamber uses as the criterion for relevance of evidence in the Judgment.

[166] *Ibid.*, p. 6.

[167] *Ibid.*, pp. 29–30.

[168] *Ibid.*, p. 6.

(2) Judicial cultural bias by omission and commission

The Defence Experts gave evidence that Mr. Ongwen's cultural milieu impacted on the interpretation of evidence.[169] The Defence objected to the cultural insensitivity in the Trial Judgment's conclusions and in Prof. W-P's and Dr. GM's evidence. These objections concerned Mr. Ongwen's food request; the language issue of the "blues" and conceptualization of mental illness in physical terms or somatization; whether those close to Mr. Ongwen would notice mental illness, and how; and Dr. GM's (and Prof. W-P's) view that mental illness would be "readily apparent" to other LRA members and fighters.[170] The Trial Chamber's cultural bias, in its responses, is illustrated by omission and commission.

(a) Judicial cultural bias by omission, Ongwen Exceptionalism and the cultural beliefs of lay witnesses

The first, and perhaps fundamental, cultural bias by omission is the Judgment's conclusion that the culture of the LRA applied to all the other abductees but not to Mr. Ongwen. The Judgment erroneously carves out this "Ongwen Exception"[171] to the toxic, and often lethal, traumatic effects of the LRA on Kony's abductees. The Judgment recounts evidence of initiation rituals, standing rules, indoctrination and Kony's brutal disciplinary regime[172] but it is silent on how these rituals and practices affected the conduct and mental state of Mr. Ongwen. The Chamber implicitly is saying that Mr. Ongwen was unaffected by the brutality and bestiality in the LRA. The "Ongwen Exception" is also inherently racist: it reduces Mr. Ongwen, a Black man, to invisibility when the Trial Chamber does not see the effects of the heinous LRA's culture on him.

[169] *See* DCB, para. 663 with footnotes to transcripts of Prof. EO and Dr. DA; Defence Notification at CR2021_04746.PDF (icc-cpi.int); Grounds of Appeal related to Culture, Grounds 30, 34, 36 and 43; DAJ, paras. 430–470; TJ: 2458–2463 (Response to Defence on cultural issues).

[170] DCB, para. 663; DAJ, paras. 451–470; *see also* TJ: 2463.

[171] *See*, DAJ, paras. 5, 380, 439–441, 380. *See also*, Beth S. Lyons, The Ongwen Chamber's Reparations Order and the "Ongwen Exception": A Concept of Dehumanization, Invisibility and Racism - Opinio Juris, 13 April 2024.

[172] TJ: 906–930.

The "Ongwen Exception" is also coupled with the Chamber's refusal to view Mr. Ongwen as a victim of the child soldier culture in the LRA.[173]

Similarly, although the Trial Chamber concludes that LRA spirituality was not a factor which contributed to the threat component relevant to duress for Mr. Ongwen,[174] there are findings in its Judgment as to Kony's spiritual power over others in the LRA.[175] This conclusion about Mr. Ongwen contradicts the evidence that Kony abused spiritualism, particularly of the Acholi people (of which Mr. Ongwen was part), to cement his power especially over vulnerable child abductees. Closely linked to this is the Chamber's refusal to consider Mr. Ongwen's abduction at the age of 8 or 9 as relevant to the charges, and especially to the defence of mental disease or defect. The Chamber bluntly stated that "Dominic Ongwen's childhood experience in the LRA is not central to the issue."[176]

The second cultural bias by omission was the Trial Chamber's failure to recognize the impact of the LRA environment and the importance of spirit possession on the lay witnesses upon whom it relies. In its methodological critique (Factor #4), the Judgment criticizes the Defence Experts for failing to corroborate their conclusions using collateral information, particularly the observations (or lack of observations) of lay witnesses.[177] First, the Chamber's allegation is not based on the evidence: the Defence Experts reviewed material, which the Detention Centre made available, and also included interviews with people close to Mr. Ongwen in the LRA in their First Report.[178] The Chamber's view is that persons close to Mr. Ongwen would notice that something was "amiss" with him and would have conveyed this information to someone, maybe an investigator or to the Court, if s/he testified. The Defence refuted this position, and at least one of the *amici* supported the Defence position that lay

---

[173] *See* section on Cultural Bias and Scientific Standards, Psychometric Testing and Malingering, subsection (1) Mr. Ongwen's social and cultural context, *infra*.

[174] TJ: 2658.

[175] TJ: 2643 *et seq.*

[176] TJ: 2592.

[177] TJ: 2545–2557.

[178] DAJ, paras. 374–380.

witnesses' observations of mental health symptoms could not and should not be relied upon.[179]

The basic problem with the Trial Chamber's premise is that it disregards and omits the immediate cultural context of the lay witness observer, which is highly relevant to what is noticed, remembered and thought to be "normal" or "abnormal." The Chamber, in its "lay witness criterion," did not factor in as important that the persons it was talking about were, like Mr. Ongwen, abductees who were forced to serve Joseph Kony in the LRA. They lived in a hostile and oppressive LRA environment under criminal rules and were subjected to punishment for showing their feelings. These lay witnesses were traumatized, and this was reflected in their observations and expressions (or lack thereof). In the culture of the LRA, abductees were trained to hide or "mask" their true feelings, especially when the feelings were perceived by Kony to be negative (wanting to escape, feeling remorse, etc.) and were punished. As the Defence Experts stated, "[e]veryone in the LRA was trained and conditioned not to mourn or show any sign of remorse....Any sign of despair, apathy and self-isolation...was 'severely punished'."[180] This also meant that their sense of "normal" and "amiss" was likely skewed by their own situations in the LRA, as well as influenced by strong beliefs in spirit possession.

Thus, the notion that lay witnesses in Mr. Ongwen's cultural environment would recognize and describe symptoms of mental illness or distress is not a logical presumption. As Prof. EO explained, women who lived with Mr. Ongwen would not have normally noticed his two different personalities, or, "if they noticed it, they probably explained it...as an experience of possession or....the after effects of battle activities, so they would regard this as normal."[181] This means that a lay witness's (lack of) observations were informed by the person's immediate context (living in a hostile LRA environment), but also in Uganda, where many hold

---

[179] *See*. DCB, paras. 630, 661–666; DAJ, paras. 381–392; *Amicus* observations of Prof. Dr. Braakman, ICC-02/04-01/15-1942 23-12-2021, Section 2.1 ("That observations made by lay persons is preferred by the Trial Chamber over the diagnosis made by professional psychiatrists is astonishing").

[180] Defence Experts' First Report, UGA-D26-0015-0004, p. 9.

[181] T-251, p. 35, ll.2–8 at CR2019_07320.PDF (icc-cpi.int); *see also* T-249, pp. 95–96 at legal-tools.org/doc/ekwo8d/pdf/.

cultural or religious beliefs in spirit possession. Prof. EO responded similarly when questioned about DSM diagnostic criterion B[182] for PTSD, and whether people around Mr. Ongwen would notice his conduct:

> I would expect they would notice... they would regard what they notice as the consequences of his involvement in... the bush or bush activities. They would interpret this as spirit possession, signs of spirit possession and they would expect that if only rituals could be conducted, Mr. Ongwen would be normal....[183]

Prof. EO also stated that Mr. Ongwen experienced dissociation in battlefield operations and that any anger, violence or frustration he expressed in this context would appear normal to others.[184] In addition, the Defence Experts explained that an individual would be able to "mask" his or her inner feelings to appear normal or function normally, so that "there should be no surprise his associates could not tell there was something amiss."[185]

How or if people observe something depends on who they are, where they come from, how they live, i.e. their cultural context or background. Their perception and expression of their observations depend on what they understand to be "normal"—which is another factor influenced by culture. As Prof. de Jong pointed out in the *Ongwen* case, what is considered "normal" or "deviant" must be determined in the context of Joseph Kony and the LRA, whether it is pathological or religious.[186] Lastly, how or if the observation is expressed also reflects culture, as well as the mental health literacy of the person.

But, in lieu of analyzing the impact of cultural factors such as spirit possession, the Trial Chamber dismissed it as "immaterial." The Judgment states:

---

[182] Criterion B is presence of intrusion symptoms associated with the traumatic event(s), beginning after the event(s) occurred. *See*, DSM-5, Posttraumatic Stress Disorder, Diagnostic Criteria, p. 271.

[183] T-251, p. 52, ll. 12–16 at CR2019_07320.PDF (icc-cpi.int).

[184] DCB, para. 632, n.1030, T-254, pp. 25–27.

[185] DCB, para. 633, n.1031, T-251, pp. 40–41.

[186] *See*, Fortuna, *An Interview with Prof. Joop de Jong*, at n.105, *supra*.

> ...the possibility that witnesses may regard symptoms of mental disorders as spirit possession is immaterial, insofar as they would still describe certain symptoms, irrespective of the cause attributed.[187]

In sum, the Trial Chamber got it wrong in its reliance on lay witnesses, due—in part—to its cultural biases: it failed to consider the "LRA culture" and also the meaning of "normality" in a setting where people believed in spirit possession or were forced into battle. Although the Chamber claimed it was not relying on lay witnesses to diagnose mental disease but only to observe any "strange" or "unexplainable" conduct by Mr. Ongwen,[188] it simply ignores that any perceptions—or absence of perceptions—had a cultural component.

(b) **Cultural bias by commission: language and food objections**

The Judgment's cultural bias is particularly evident in its outright characterization and dismissal of (1) Mr. Ongwen's food request for termites (*ngwen*, meaning "white ants" in Acholi, a Ugandan delicacy) which Dr. DA testified was a serious request, and not a joke, as suggested by the Prosecution; and (2) Dr. DA's evidence that there was no word for "blues" or "feeling blue" in many African languages as "trivial and without any serious link to the issue under consideration."[189]

The Trial Chamber's response is problematic on a number of fronts. First, the term "trivial," like the use of "immaterial" in the Judgment in

---

[187] TJ: 2501.

[188] TJ: para. 2499. Based on the evidence from Prof. W-P, the Trial Chamber observed that no witness who was in a position to observe Dominic Ongwen 2002–2005 gave testimony that s/he noticed anything "strange" or "unexplainable" in his conduct. The Appeals Chamber repeats and re-explains this in the AJ: 1246, stating: "What was important was whether these lay persons recognized and reported any unusual behaviour that would have assisted the Trial Chamber in assessing whether Mr. Ongwen suffered from a mental disease at the material time."

[189] TJ: 2463 reads (in part):

> The Defence pointed to five specific issues which—it appears—would indicate the superiority of the Defence experts' assessments over those of Prosecution Experts in this context. Two of these, that is the interpretation of Dominic Ongwen's request for termites as a serious food request rather than a joke and the absence of the word "blues" in "many African languages", are trivial and without any serious link to the issue under consideration...

See generally, AJ: 1311–1340 affirming TJ, and particularly AJ: 1332–1339.

respect to spirit possession, connotes insignificance—which certainly is a poor word choice to describe cultural issues related to food and language. But it is as troubling that these points were deemed irrelevant because there was no "serious link" to the "charged period." This very narrow idea of relevance, or what makes something "non-trivial," communicates that cultural factors do not matter. The food request was about Mr. Ongwen wanting to eat culturally familiar food. It should have been relevant to the Trial Chamber if it was trying to holistically understand the individual, Dominic Ongwen, who is sitting as a defendant before it—day after day, year after year—and not simply within a specified time of the "charged period," which started almost up to two decades earlier.

Second, the fact that there is no word for "blues" in African languages should have been relevant and central to the Trial Chamber's reliance on lay witness observations as a determinant factor in its assessment of whether Mr. Ongwen was suffering from a mental illness or disease. If there are no words in a language to describe something, or the words mean something specific based on a particular culture, then this information is highly relevant, especially in a Western-based court, such as the ICC, located in The Hague. The evidence of Dr. DA indicates that how or if a person perceives what may be wrong, and communicates this (or doesn't communicate this) are all cultural factors that must be taken into account by a Trial Chamber. Prof. EO's testimony about the somatization and spiritualization of mental illness in Uganda and other parts of Africa suggests that if a patient communicates or observes something, how it is presented is culture-bound. Yet, the Chamber "wrote off" the cultural significance of language in the example of "the blues" as trivial and also failed to consider that mental illnesses were somatized in Uganda.[190]

The Trial Chamber relied on whether lay persons perceived that something was "awry" with Mr. Ongwen, and disregarded the point that whether they even noticed would be triggered by their understanding of what is abnormal or unhealthy. Their perceptions, and whether a word existed to express a feeling, were thus determined by culture. These cultural biases by commission impacted on whether lay witnesses would be reliable as a collateral source of information (Factor #4).

---

[190] DCB, para. 663, n.1073 and n.1074; TJ: 2463; DAJ, paras 459–470.

The Trial Chamber's response to the Defence objections on cultural issues displayed a bias in respect to the Defence Experts' evidence. The Judgment interpreted these issues to reflect the "superiority of the Defence Experts' assessments over those of Prosecution experts in this context."[191] The Judgment's phrasing of the Defence Experts' "superiority" sets a wrong and harmful paradigm. There is no evidence that the Defence Experts expressed a view of "superiority." To the contrary, the Defence Experts testified that Mr. Ongwen's cultural milieu impacted on the interpretation of the evidence. This interpretation had to consider the impact of, and make adjustments for, other factors (culture, how questions are asked, how questions are understood, etc.). Significantly, the Judgment's view of "superiority" conveyed a framework in which Prof. W-P's misrepresentation that the Defence Experts held the view that non-African professionals could not diagnose African patients in Africa was acceptable and conveniently fit.

In tandem with its false "superiority paradigm," the Trial Chamber sought to defend and rehabilitate the two Prosecution Experts, Prof. W-P and Dr. GM, as a predicate issue before presenting its conclusions about the mental disease defence in the Judgment.[192] The Defence appealed the Judgment's conclusion that these Prosecution Experts did not ignore or dismiss cultural factors.[193] It is true that Dr. GM mentioned culture and transcultural psychiatry in her testimony and that she worked with people from many different cultures.[194] But these are not "credentials" which automatically make one immune from cultural bias.[195] The issue is whether and how the mental health professional integrates notions of culture into her or his mental health/illness analysis. Both Prof. W-P and Dr. GM appear to have done this in the *Al Hassan* case but definitely did not do this in the *Ongwen* case.

[191] TJ: 2463. *See*, DCB, para. 663.

[192] TJ: 2458–2463; DCB, paras. 661, 665

[193] DAJ (Ground 30), paras. 451–458.

[194] T-162, p. 10, ll.17–25 to p. 11, l. 1–4; T-163, p. 41, ll. 24–25 to p. 42, ll.1–11.

[195] *See*, Ana Antic, n.40 *supra* (citing examples of racism in the conceptualization of cultural psychiatry and that there is a political spectrum within cultural psychiatry).

In sum, by missing the importance of the cultural context, especially its impact on mental illness—the Trial Chamber made mistakes: it ended up adopting a position which discounted the importance of affirmatively considering cultural factors in its Judgment.[196]

Cultural Bias and Scientific Standards, Psychometric Testing and Malingering

The Trial Chamber's cultural bias is alive and well in its critique of the Defence Experts for failing to apply "scientifically validated methods and tools" (Factor #2). This prong of the methodology critique played out in many of the issues addressed in litigation, including substantive analysis of Mr. Ongwen's mental illnesses. One of the most significant areas was the issue of malingering, and whether the Defence Experts' assessment and opinion was based on "standards" within the profession.[197]

The Trial Chamber was fixated on one specific diagnostic tool for malingering—a psychometric test as *the* "scientific tool" for diagnosis. The Defence Experts explained that they had made an assessment and evaluation of Mr. Ongwen, based on their expertise and clinical interviews with him and concluded that testing him for malingering was not warranted.[198] But the Trial Chamber refused to credit their expert opinions. Dr. GM criticized the Defence Experts and Prof. de Jong for not challenging Mr. Ongwen's malingering and for adopting an "incredulous and uncritical approach."[199]

In fact, the Trial Chamber gives the impression that the Defence Experts opposed the use of psychometric tests, period. This is not true. Prof. EO testified that psychometric tests are useful but that their utility

[196] Judges can not be expected to be experts on a particular mental illness and its cultural roots and expression. But, they can be expected to recognize when cultural factors raise the "red flag" of reasonable doubt—for example, when the cultural component affects how or even if symptoms are noticed, and whether they are interpreted as "abnormal" behavior.

[197] On malingering (Methodology Factor #5), *see generally* DCB, paras. 667–673; TJ: 2558–2568; DAJ, paras. 393–409.

[198] DCB, paras. 667–673.

[199] DCB, para. 609 (n.996 Dr. Mezey's Expert Report, UGA-OTP-0280-0786, paras. 43 and 81 [Defence Experts' reports criticized as "extremely credulous"]).

is based on the specific circumstances. He hoped that the fact that they had not used them would not invalidate their observations.[200] Dr. DA had authored a test for use in Uganda on depression, the Akena Visual Depression Inventory (AViDI-18), as a valid screen for depression in patients with low literacy and who had limited or no mental health literacy.[201] So, the idea that either Defence Expert was "anti-psychometric tests" is baseless.

Yet, the Prosecution Experts Prof. W-P and Dr. GM spearheaded the campaign that Mr. Ongwen was a malingerer, was "faking" his symptoms and illnesses and that anything he self-reported should be discounted. The Trial Chamber did just that. It found "…the way in which they [Defence Experts] dismissed malingering as a possible explanation for the presence of symptoms of mental disorders apparent from the self-report of Dominic Ongwen unconvincing and considers this to be a major factor militating against reliance on their reports."[202] Interestingly, the three Experts who had interviewed Mr. Ongwen—the Defence Experts and the Court-Appointed Expert—rejected the malingering diagnosis of two of the Prosecution Experts, who had not interviewed Mr. Ongwen. The third, Dr. Abbo, took no position on this issue, although it appeared that she relied on the clinical interviews of the Defence Experts and the Court-Appointed Expert in her Expert Report.

What reasonably should have been framed as a difference of professional opinion on malingering, morphed into a touchstone for rejecting the Defence Experts' evidence. The Trial Chamber, again uncritically, simply latched onto this notion: it suggested that if the Defence Experts had used "proper" scientific methodology, they would have reached a different conclusion, i.e. that Mr. Ongwen was malingering. Thus, the failure to do cognitive testing for malingering became a central factor in the Chamber's "methodology critique."

---

[200] T-254, p. 12, ll. 24–25 to p. 13, ll. 1–23.

[201] *See*, Dickens Akena, John Joska and Dan J. Stein, Sensitivity and specificity of the Akena Visual Depression Inventory (AViDI-18) in Kampala (Uganda) and Cape Town (South Africa), 121 BR. J. PSYCHIATRY 301-307 (2018) (validated the Akena Visual Depression Inventory [AViDI] as a good psychometric tool and for use to screen for depression in settings with higher rates of illiteracy).

[202] TJ: 2568.

(1) Mr. Ongwen's social and cultural context

First, the Judgment's cultural bias is illustrated by its ignorance and/or disregard for the social and cultural context of Mr. Ongwen, as an abductee in the LRA and an Acholi from Northern Uganda. There is a plethora of evidence of the trauma and mental illnesses of child soldiers, and the Trial Chamber's conclusions simply overlooked or rejected this. As Dr. Braakman, one of the *amici curiae*, wrote: "Based purely on statistics it is very unlikely that the accused did **not** suffer from any mental disorder. Nine out of ten former child soldiers in Uganda suffer from depressed mood in adulthood. And, that is just of one of several possible mental health consequences..."[203] (bold in the original).

Second, the Trial Chamber, through its "Ongwen Exception" analysis, rejected that Mr. Ongwen was a victim of the LRA's "child soldier culture."[204] Based on the Chamber's "Ongwen Exception,"[205] this culture had no impact on his mental state or conduct, as a child abductee and did not have any effect on Mr. Ongwen after he reached 18, the age of culpability in Article 26 of the Rome Statute.[206] The Judgment held that Mr. Ongwen's age of abduction at 8 or 9 was not relevant to crimes for which he was convicted when he was over 18.[207]

The *Ongwen* Chamber's view of child soldiering, compared to the *Lubanga* Chamber's view, illustrates the inconsistent judicial narratives of child soldiering at the ICC. As Mark Drumbl points out, "*Lubanga* cast the linkage between the past as a child soldier and the present as a former child soldier as linear and continuous....Once a child soldier in fact, always a child soldier in mind, body, and soul. In *Ongwen,* however, the

---

[203] ICC-02/04-01/15-1942 23-12-2021, Section 2.1, p. 6.

[204] The term, "child soldier culture," is used by Noelle Higgins in reference to the *Ongwen* case. *See*, INTERSECTIONS OF LAW AND CULTURE AT THE INTERNATIONAL CRIMINAL COURT ('INTERSECTIONS'), Julie Fraser and Brianne McGonigle Leyh, editors, Edward Elgar Publishing: UK and US, 2021, p. 239.

[205] *See* section on Culture, Mental Health and Implicit Bias, sub-section (2)(a) Judicial cultural bias by omission, Ongwen Exceptionalism and cultural beliefs of lay witnesses *supra* on "Ongwen Exception."

[206] *See*, Charles A. Taku and Beth S. Lyons, The *Ongwen* Judgments: A Stain on International Justice, J. INT. CRIM. JUSTICE, 2024, mqae044, https://doi.org/10.1093/jicj/mqae044.

[207] TJ: 27, 2592.

linkage between the accused's past as a child soldier and his present as a former child soldier was seen as discontinuous and contingent…."[208] He concludes that the different narratives[209] on child soldiering in the two cases promote inconsistency and unpredictability in international criminal law.[210]

The "disconnect" between Mr. Ongwen, the child soldier abductee and Mr. Ongwen, the "adult" (over 18) child soldier supports the analyses of Mr. Ongwen as victim turned perpetrator, and other variations of this construct, including Erin Baines' "complex political perpetrator."[211] These formulations run counter to the Defence position – once a victim, always a victim.

Third, the Trial Chamber "missed" the whole cultural context of the "Situation in Uganda," which is how the court officer called the *Ongwen* case at the start of each court session. The Chamber simply did not understand and/or rejected the effects of decades of war and conflict, resulting in mass trauma on everyone, including Mr. Ongwen.

Seggane Musisi, a professor of psychiatry at Makerere University in Kampala, testified as a Victims' Expert (PCV-0003) about the relation between Acholi culture and traditions, PTSD and trauma. Yet, the Trial Chamber rejected his evidence as irrelevant to its deliberations about Mr. Ongwen because "it does not directly underlie any part of the Chamber's analysis as to whether the facts alleged in the charges are established."[212] It is baffling that the Chamber could not "connect" the significance of

---

[208] Shifting Narratives: Ongwen and Lubanga on the Effects of Child Soldiering | Justice in Conflict, 20 April 2016.

[209] The importance of the narrative, especially in international criminal cases, cannot be emphasized enough. As a former ICTY Prosecutor, Professor Sir Geoffrey Nice, has pointed out "[t]he struggle for the interpretation of historical events through the trial record might be as important in [the] long run as the determination of guilt or innocence of the individuals tried." Legal Process as a Tool to Rewrite History – Law, Politics, History, Lecture, Gresham College, 13 February 2013. *See also*, Richard Ashby Wilson, *Writing History in International Criminal Trials* (Cambridge University Press: New York, 2011).

[210] While Drumbl's observations were based on Pre-Trial Chamber II's COC Decision, available at the time of his writing in 2016, they are confirmed years later in the *Ongwen* Trial and Appeal Judgments.

[211] Erin K. Baines, *Complex political perpetrators: reflections on Dominic Ongwen*, J. MOD. AFR. STUD., 47, 2 (Cambridge University Press, 2009), pp. 163–191.

[212] TJ: 602; DAJ, paras. 213, 435–441.

Acholi culture and PTSD to the *Ongwen* mental disease defence: Mr. Ongwen was part of the Acholi people, and PTSD was one of the mental illnesses he was struggling with in the LRA and continues to struggle with today.

As Musisi and Kinyanda[213] have concluded, "trauma, especially war-related mass trauma, is endemic and enigmatic in Africa stretching over 600 years." They cite research over the past two or so decades which documents the "horrendous trauma and stressor-related mental health sequels, following the never ending enigmatic war-trauma on the African continent."[214] These conclusions provide an important social, political and cultural contextual framework for all the prosecutions at the ICC, which—for the last twenty+ years—have been against African defendants. In essence, the ICC "situations" are ground zero for mental illness—where situation countries are either in a post-conflict stage or, more likely, in an ongoing and continuing conflict stage.[215]

In *Ongwen*, the plethora of literature on the impact of war, and especially being a child soldier, on both children and adults, was augmented by the testimony of many witnesses. Dr. DA vividly described the early trauma of Mr. Ongwen in the first few months when he was abducted as a child of 8 or 9:

> The trauma was related to skinning of people alive, being forced to carry the heads of severed persons and dumping them into a pit. Having the intestines of people hung up on walls. The trauma was related to bludgeoning of little children who had tried to escape and had been brought back.

---

[213] Seggane Musisi and Eugene Kinyanda, *Long-term Impact of War, Civil War, and Persecution in Civilian Populations—Conflict and Post-Traumatic Stress in African Communities*, FRONT. PSYCHIATRY, 11:20, doi: https://doi.org/10.3389/psyt.2020.00020. *See also*, discussion of Dr. Musisi's evidence at DCB, para. 539; TJ: 602, 2579; DAJ, paras. 434–438; AJ: 1299–1306.

[214] *Ibid.*, pp. 3, 15.

[215] I am not saying that people living on the African continent are "more prone" to trauma and mental illness than those living in war and conflict zones outside of Africa. Nor am I arguing that everyone in a war and conflict area develops mental illness. But, the general negative impact of war and conflict on mental health has cultural components in every society, and recognizing the specific history of a region is important to understand the mental health consequences which exist.

> The events were bad. That was the context in which the traumatic events happened.[216]

Major (ret.) Pollar Awich (D-0133), a Defence Expert on child soldiers, gave evidence that the trauma of child soldiers never ends and that Mr. Ongwen did not have a "mind of his own" because child abductees were so indoctrinated and brutalized in the LRA.[217] Major Awich understands, from his own experience, what happened to child soldiers: he was abducted as a child by the National Resistance Army ('NRA') in the 1980s—the predecessor of the UPDF. He was then recruited into the UPDF and maintains his rank as a Major (ret.) today.[218] In addition, he worked with ex-child soldiers in Uganda and was elected twice to the UN Committee on the Rights of the Child in Geneva. But, the Trial Chamber, while accepting Major Awich's experiences as credible, also rejected his expert conclusions on the enduring effects of being a child soldier.[219]

(2) **The Gulu Study—war, children and mental illness**

The evidence of the Defence Expert on child soldiers, the Victims' Expert and the Expert in *Lubanga*, as well as others at trial,[220] is

---

[216] T-249, pp 103–104. 969 at legal-tools.org/doc/ekwo8d/pdf/.

[217] D-133, T-203, p. 64, ll. 11–21, p. 75, ln. 25 to p. 76, l. 10.

[218] TJ: 612; DCB, para. 577, *see also*, paras. 566–567, 572, 621, 693, 724–725; DAJ, paras. 611–615.

[219] TJ: 612. *See*, T-203, p. 78, l. 2 to p. 79, l. 7 (D-0133 testimony on persistence over time of psychological and physical phenomena in [former] child soldiers, including PTSD).

[220] The longevity of the effects of being a child soldier is also a conclusion of other experts. For example, in the *Ongwen* case, Victims's Expert PCV-2 concludes that children abducted by the LRA suffered from long-term consequences in many areas, and that the long-term harm was enabled by the intergenerational transmission of trauma. *See*, Executive Summary at UGA-PCV-00020-0081, from "The Consequences of the Abduction of Children Under 15: Implications for Individuals, Families, Communities, and Acholi Society," a detailed Expert Report ((UGA-PCV-0002-0076) by Michael G. Wessells, PhD.

See also, Expert Report by Elizabeth Schauer, PhD a Court-Appointed Expert in *Lubanga*. Her report, "The Psychological Impact of Child Soldiering," ICC-01/04-01/06- 1729-Anx 1. 25-020 2009, which was submitted into evidence by the *Ongwen* Defence, is available at https://www.legaltools.org/doc/ccb0d2/pdf. Dr. Schauer also details the long-term effects of trauma in the child soldiers' experience, including PTSD, *which persists, according to one study, up to 40 years after the trauma* (Schauer Report, p. 15) and describes the effects on individuals, and their families and communities, noting the transgenerational effects. (italics added)

supported by Ugandan researchers. There is at least one study which appears to be factually identical to the situation in *Ongwen*, and likely researched coterminous to the "charged period."[221] It is entitled "Psychiatric disorders among war-abducted and non-abducted adolescents in Gulu district, Uganda: a comparative study."[222]

There were two general conclusions: (1) "war-abducted children are significantly more affected psychologically and therefore should be screened and assessed for psychiatric problems;" (2) "majority of children and adolescents in war affected areas have multiple and clinically significant emotional responses to different kinds of traumatic exposure with a high incidence of major depression; generalized anxiety disorder; PTSD; and co-morbidity."[223] The authors of the study explain that one of its limitations was its reliance on Western-oriented questionnaires and methodology.[224]

The researchers note that the Gulu district had "the longest and most severe experience of the 18-year-old LRA insurgency" and has the largest number of IDP camps, where about 436,239 persons are living.[225] This is the same area where Mr. Ongwen is from. The overwhelming majority of persons in the study were, like Mr. Ongwen, Acholi (91.5% of the abducted group; 95.8% of the non-abducted group). The most significant traumatic experiences were predominantly direct, that is, forced to kill, being forced to perform rituals, being forced to torture and forced to leave home and property.[226]

---

[221] The "charged period" refers to the period of the indictment charges, 2002–2005. The Gulu Study was likely conducted during the charged period, since the paper was received 23 October 2006, and accepted in 12 March 2007 and published in November, 2007.

[222] J. Okello, T.S. Onen and S. Musisi, *Psychiatric disorders among war-abducted and non-abducted adolescents in Gulu district, Uganda: a comparative study*, 10(4) AFR. J. PSYCHIATRY 225-231 (2007).

[223] *Ibid.*, p. 230.

[224] *Ibid.*, p. 229: Several potential limitations of this study are recognized: "The current study is limited by the reliance on Western oriented questionnaires and lack of a locally developed traumatic events checklist and instrument to measure potentially confounding socio-demographic factors. It should be noted that non abducted adolescents were still significantly exposed to the events of war through their relatives and the media."

[225] *Ibid.*, p. 226.

[226] *Ibid.*, p. 228. The Trial Judgment draws a similar conclusion in terms of the traumatic experiences of LRA abductees (TJ: 906–930), but does not include Mr. Ongwen. The Judgment creates an "Ongwen Exception" and gives no reasons. *See*, DAJ, paras. 440–441.

Using the MINI KID psychiatric disorder criteria, 70.7% of the abducted group met the criteria for one or more disorders compared to 43.7% of non-abducted group. These disorders included major depression, suicidality, PTSD and others (both individually and in co-morbidity, i.e. PTSD and major depression disorder). These are among the same diagnoses which the Defence Experts and the Court-Appointed Expert made about Mr. Ongwen.

The study found a discrepancy between higher rates of psychiatric disorder (70.7% among abducted adolescents) and the rates of general psychological distress (51.2%), and concluded that diagnosis of a disorder does not "always suggest severe functional impairment...."[227] It concluded that "good social adaptation is possible even in the presence of psychopathology or following multiple traumas."[228]

(3) **Functionality and mental illness**

For the *Ongwen* case, the conclusions in the Gulu Study that mental illness can co-exist with functionality are extremely significant. They support a fundamental premise advanced by the Defence that mental illness and functionality can co-exist.[229] They also refute the findings of the Trial Judgment and Prof. W-P and Dr. GM that Mr. Ongwen's ability to function in battle, or make decisions was evidence that he was not mentally ill.

The functionality premise was a key part of the Prosecution's narrative: Mr. Ongwen was a "success" story in the LRA, rising up through the ranks to higher leadership positions. This narrative ignores the different ways in which child soldiers have coped with their adverse and hostile environment[230] and Mr. Ongwen's struggles in the LRA, where he was punished on several occasions in LRA prisons when he tried to escape.[231]

---

[227] *Ibid.*, p. 229.

[228] *Ibid.*, p. 229.

[229] *See*, DCB, paras. 637–650 (Prosecution Myth #2: Those who suffer from mental illness are dysfunctional).

[230] *See*, for example, Victims' Expert Dr. Wessels on resiliency at DCB, para. 644, n.1045.

[231] DAJ, para. 440, n.508 – Prof de Jong's Report documents five failed escape attempts made by Mr. Ongwen while in the LRA. *See also*, Defence Experts' First Report, references to escape attempts in n.508.

The idea that a person who has a mental disease is dysfunctional contradicts the evidence that mental diseases do not present or expose their symptoms 24/7.[232] I think the Trial Judges observed Mr. Ongwen over a period of years, almost daily, and concluded that he appeared "normal" and "functional." This assessment could not have considered the fact that Mr. Ongwen at whom they were looking was medicated for his mental illnesses throughout the trial process. This factor also ensured that Mr. Ongwen could be present in court each day.

Thus, Mr. Ongwen rarely exhibited mental distress in a visible manner in open court during a total of almost six years of trial proceedings.[233] In these very few instances, he was reacting, based on deep-seated trauma: one was during the testimony of Expert witness Dr. GM, who appeared to Mr. Ongwen to be Joseph Kony, and another was during the testimony of a Prosecution witness, when Mr. Ongwen learned—for the first time—that the UPDF was responsible for the death of his brother, and, lastly, when there was testimony about the killing of his parents. These few visible occurrences were within a larger context in which, no doubt, Mr. Ongwen was constantly being re-traumatized as he listened to testimony and re-lived his life in the LRA.[234]

In sum, in its Judgment, the Trial Chamber substituted its own observations of Mr. Ongwen for the professional opinions of the Defence and Court-Appointed Experts. These in-court observations of a defendant, whose mental illnesses were being medicated, pre-disposed them to a finding that Mr. Ongwen was not mentally ill, during the "charged period."

---

[232] DCB, paras. 622–636 ("Prosecution Myth #1: Mental illness, including severe mental illness is visible 24/7 to anyone observing but especially those closest to the person affected")

[233] I am excluding the constant periods of disassociation, which were not recorded in the transcript. As Mr. Ongwen explained to the Trial Chamber at the Sentencing Hearing and to the Appeals Chamber, he only understood about 40% of the proceedings and did not understand 60% of what was said. *See*, Sentencing Hearing, ICC-02/04-01/15-T-261-ENG ET WT (April 15, 2021), p. 4, ll. 8–14, CR2021_03573.PDF (icc-cpi.int); Appeals Hearing, ICC-02/04-01/15-T-267-ENG ET WT (Feb. 18, 2022), p. 35, ll. 5-7, CR2022_01626.PDF (icc-cpi.int).

[234] The trial started in early December 2016 and ended in March 2020. The Judgment and Sentence were rendered in February and May 2021, respectively. The Appeals Judgment was rendered in December 2022.

(4) Malingering: psychometric testing is not a litmus test

The Trial Chamber did not consider Mr. Ongwen's cultural context in its conclusions about malingering. Prosecution Expert Dr. GM testified that it was difficult to fake illnesses over long periods of time and that this required a level of knowledge of the illnesses and their symptoms.[235] The logical question is: how could Mr. Ongwen, a child soldier in the bush, constantly under surveillance and control by Joseph Kony and isolated from the outside world, learn about mental illnesses and their symptoms. Yet, the Trial Chamber fails to address or explain how Mr. Ongwen could have "faked" the symptoms for his multiple mental illnesses which were diagnosed: major depressive disorder (MDD), PTSD, dissociative identity disorder and dissociative amnesia, suicide ideation and symptoms of obsessive-compulsive disorder.

However, the diagnostic use of psychometric tests is a key component of the Judgment's cultural bias in its methodology critique, especially for malingering.[236] Psychometric tests are cognitive tests that are used in many areas of life (employment, for example), not just in forensic psychiatry. Cognitive tests reflect implicit cultural bias. Psychometric testing has come under scrutiny for decades within the profession, because the tests themselves, as well as the conditions under which they are administered by the examiner and received or understood by the examinee, are fraught with cultural issues.[237] In addition to cultural bias, these tests have also been criticized for producing inaccurate and ineffective results.

First, as Gerald Young and Eric Y. Drogin discuss, there is no accepted definition of malingering, with base rate or prevalence estimates varying from 1% to over 50%.[238] They point out, for example, that "faking bad" could be confused with malingering and that terms such as

[235] DCB, para. 670 ("... It's quite difficult, unless you have read a lot of books, are very clever and are very persistent.....to fake convincingly over a period of time. *You can occasionally produce symptoms that look like mental illness, but to maintain that is impossible.*[1091]") (italics added)

[236] The Trial Judgment discusses malingering, Methodology Factor #5, at paras. 2532, 2558–2568.

[237] With any "standardized" tests, the fairness and equity of the testing mechanism is at stake. This includes multiple levels of cultural concerns: between the examiner and examinee, as well as the content of the tests and the forms in which questions are presented and the answers are accepted.

[238] Gerald Young and Eric Y. Drogin, *Psychological Injury and Law I: Causality, malingering and PTSD*, 3 (2) MENTAL HEALTH L. & POL'Y J. 373 (Spring 2014).

overreporting, exaggeration of symptoms, factitious presentations and others have specific definitions and need to be used more precisely by researchers. This means that "faking bad" (the term used by Dr. GM to describe Mr. Ongwen's malingering) is not the same thing as malingering.

Second, there is the problem of the accuracy of the tests and rate of false positives, for example, in the Miller Forensic Assessment of Symptoms (M-FAST) test.[239] Even when tests are indicated, they can lead to false conclusions where overreporting or exaggeration of symptoms may have many sources, not only malingering.[240]

The issue of accuracy of diagnosis is further compounded by cultural bias in the tests, which can result in false diagnoses. Yoram Braw discusses the link between cultural biases in tests and the risk of persons being diagnosed falsely with malingering.[241] He notes that research in the field is still limited (Braw's article was published in 2021) and has tended to focus on English-speaking minorities in Western countries.[242] He also points out how "culture bound syndromes" such as *ataque de nervios*—a

---

[239] The Miller Forensic Assessment of Symptoms Test (M-FAST) is a screening measure for use in a forensic setting to detect malingering and uses seven scales to make the assessment. Walczyk et al. report that "…a third of the scales on the M-FAST have low internal consistency, resulting in low reliability for these scales. Vitacco et al. (notes omitted) found '…an unacceptably high of false positives (10%) using the total scale scores.'" From Jeffrey J, Walczyk, Nate Sewell and Meghan B. DiBenedetto, *A Review of Approaches to Detecting Malingering in Forensic Contexts and Promising Cognitive Load-Inducing Lie Detection Techniques*, 9 FRONT. PSYCHIATRY, Article 700, 4 (2018).

[240] *See*, Harald Merckelbach, Brechji Dandachi-FitzGerald, Daniel van Helvoort, Marko Jelicic and Henry Otgaar, *When Patients Overreport Symptoms: More Than Just Malingering*, Vol. 28(3) CURR. DIR. PSYCHOL. SCI. 321–326 (2019), https://doi.org/10.1177/0963721419837681. The authors point out that overreporting of symptoms by patients has a number of sources (of which one is malingering) and that to conclude that malingering is the cause of symptom exaggeration in symptom-validity tests such as SIMS and TOMM, may result in misleading conclusions. They conclude that the "predominant view on symptom overreporting is that it indicates malingering….however, as our review shows, there are multiple pathways to symptom overreporting and malingering is only one of these…" (p. 324).

[241] Yoram Braw, *Cultural Aspects in Assessing Malingering Detection*, Chapter, July 2021, ResearchGate, pp. 181–183. In: A. M. Horton, Jr. and C.R. Reynolds (eds), DETECTION OF MALINGERING DURING HEAD INJURY LITIGATION, 177–200, Springer, Cham. https://doi.org/10.1007/978-3-030-54656-4_3. Braw discusses the Reliable Digit Span (RDS) test. He notes that in one study, in the United States, the RDS scores of Hispanics were significantly lower than those of Caucasians and "they were therefore at increased risk of being erroneously labeled as malingerers based on established cutoffs, suggesting that adjustment of the RDS is in order when assessing Hispanics." (internal references omitted). He states that whether this finding can be generalized to other groups, however, is unclear and necessitates further research.

[242] Braw, p. 182 (all references *infra.* to ResearchGate paper)

syndrome in which an individual may exhibit extreme anxiety and even suicidal gestures, but then returns to a normal state of functioning a short time later—may be erroneously interpreted as indicating malingering.[243] While Braw argues that malingering likely crosses cultural and ethnic divides, this indicates that there is a corresponding need for cross-culturally valid instruments for its detection. Braw also discusses other cognitive tests and how cultural bias affects usage and diagnoses for malingering.

Lastly, the level of education has been shown to affect test results. A study of Colombian adults where the Test of Memory Malingering (TOMM) was used, concluded that although the TOMM can be used cross-culturally with literate individuals, adults with lower literacy rates performed significantly worse, raising concerns regarding the use of this test with educationally diverse samples.[244]

Yet, despite the evidence that the tests used are plagued with problems on many fronts, especially cultural bias, the Judgment appears to be almost obsessed with psychometric testing as the "gold standard" for diagnostic tools in psychiatry—regardless of the debate and controversies in the profession. But, this "gold standard" has been and continues to be deeply tarnished.

The debate over culture and its impact on cognitive tests has been raging for decades. As Braw points out, "interest in the effects of cultural factors on cognitive testing has been noted since the 1980s, with the literature growing rapidly since the 1990s (Ardila, 2007, p. 24)."[245] He concludes that "...culture impacts performance on cognitive tests either directly or indirectly" and cites language proficiency and education as indirect factors which impact on test results.[246]

Alfredo Ardila has explored the thesis that culture can affect neuropsychological testing and that cognitive testing is governed by implicit cultural rules. He states that "culture refers to the set of learned traditions

---

[243] Braw, p. 183.

[244] Alicia Nijdam-Jones, Diego Rivera, Barry Rosenfeld, Juan Carlos Arango-Lasprilla, *The effect of literacy and culture on cognitive effort test performance: An examination of the Test of Memory Malingering in Colombia*, 41(10) J. CLIN. EXP. NEUROPSYCHOL. 1015–1023 (2019).

[245] Braw, p. 178.

[246] *Ibid.*, p. 179.

and living styles, shared by the members of a society…the minimal definition of culture could simply be, *culture is the specific way of living of a human group*."[247] (italics in original). In his analysis of cultural values in psychometric testing, he concludes that cognitive testing relies on a set of cultural values which cannot be regarded as universal and that psychometric cognitive testing is "only appropriate in those societies with a solid psychometric tradition, basically, Western societies. In other societies, behavioral scales and more qualitative approaches should be preferred."[248]

Ardila points out further that

> Psychometric tests have been developed in some specific cultures, and are strongly biased by the modal culture values observed in these cultures. Nonetheless, these specific values and behavior styles do not necessarily represent universal values and behaviors. Understanding these cultural assumptions, and developing assessment procedures correctly tailored to other cultures, represents a major endeavor for twenty first century neuropsychology.[249]

The take-away for the *Ongwen* case is that the Trial Chamber's insistence that a psychometric test for malingering should have been administered by the Defence Experts is, in judicial parlance, misplaced. It also exhibits a profound disrespect for the Defence Experts' professional judgment in their choice of method to assess whether Mr. Ongwen was malingering, and it overlooks the cultural bias in the existing psychometric instruments to evaluate malingering, as well as the incidence of inaccuracies.

In the context of this ongoing debate about the impact of culture on cognitive tests, the Trial Chamber—without reservation and without caution—wrongly concluded that the Defence Experts did not use scientific methods, particularly to assess malingering, based on Prof. W-P's view that psychometric testing was the "gold standard" for diagnostic tools in psychiatry. Its adoption of psychometric testing as a litmus test

[247] Alfredo Ardila, *Cultural Values Underlying Psychometric Cognitive Testing*, 15(4) NEUROPSYCHOL. REV., 185–95, 185 (Dec 2005), DOI: https://doi.org/10.1007/s11065-005-9180-y.

[248] *Ibid.*, p. 192.

[249] *Ibid.*, p. 193.

for malingering—with no *caveats* as to possible cultural implications—based on the culturally biased evidence of Prof. W-P, rendered the Judgment's conclusions biased.

There were definitely professional differences over the choice of diagnostic tools to use with Mr. Ongwen, including to determine whether he was malingering or not.[250] But the Trial Chamber turned these differences into a *raison d'être* to completely reject the Defence Experts' evidence.[251] The Chamber's cultural blindspots prevented it from applying the correct legal principle of proof beyond a reasonable doubt in assessing whether the Prosecution had met its burden of proof in the methodology critique.

Lastly, it is important to note that the Trial Chamber's methodology critique, with its emphasis on testing—particularly psychometric testing—as the sole credible scientific instrument, appears to contradict its reliance on observations of lay persons, with no training at all in identifying mental illness (Factor #4). The Judgment juxtaposes two factors: an "objective" testing tool for diagnosis and the "subjective" observations of lay persons. This also underscores that the Chamber selectively chose factors upon which it would rely, without rigorous scrutiny of its own methodology and approach, for consistency.

(5) **Assessing mental illness**

Granted, looking backward to the period 2002–2005 more than a decade and one-half later is not an exact science. But it certainly becomes a guessing game if the origins of the mental illnesses are not even considered. In *Ongwen,* the Trial Chamber refused to consider the initial traumatic event which permanently affected and changed Mr. Ongwen's mental status—his abduction by the LRA when he was a child.[252]

This error was compounded by the Trial Chamber's view that mental illness must be analyzed and assessed exclusively between 2002 and 2005 (the "charged period"). Mental illness is not static, and it does not fit

[250] DCB, paras. 651–653, 667–673; TJ: 2565.

[251] DAJ, paras. 342–350.

[252] TJ: 27, 2592.

neatly into a "time box." Nor does mental illness display its symptoms 24/7. Even Prof. W-P explained that mental illness fluctuates over time.[253] In the *Al Hassan* case, he and Dr. GM recognized that "mental fitness" is not a static state.[254] This operational reality of mental illness necessitates that the determination of whether mental illness exists must be made on a continuum: mental illness cannot be confined to a specific period. Mental illness does not start and stop on a particular calendar schedule. Hence, its origins and development in Mr. Ongwen precede the "charged period" and continue long after the period ends. Thus, the Trial Chamber's efforts to "pigeon-hole" evidence of Mr. Ongwen's mental illness into 2002–2005 run counter to how mental illness operates.

The Trial Chamber's rejection of the evidence of its Court-Appointed Expert, Prof. de Jong, also illustrates its dismissal of any historical information relevant to Mr. Ongwen's mental status at the time his Report was requested, in late 2016, at the beginning of the trial.[255] Prof. de Jong diagnosed Mr. Ongwen with severe PTSD, severe MDD and other specified dissociative disorder.[256] These diagnoses were also among those made by the Defence Experts. In its Judgment, the Chamber uses the "charged period" to reject Prof. de Jong's evidence. It states that the Report was prepared to examine Mr. Ongwen's mental health during the trial and "not at the time of his conduct relevant under the charges, [thus] the Chamber does not consider that it can rely on that report directly for its conclusions with respect to the issue at hand [referring to the Article 31(1)(a) defence]."[257]

(6) **The use and abuse of "the charged period"**

Throughout the *Ongwen* Judgment, "the charged period" is a ubiquitous reference point. The "charged period"—between July 2002 and December 2005—is the time span or temporal jurisdiction of the charges

---

[253] DCB, para. 623, n.1015.

[254] *Al Hassan* Report, para. 238.

[255] TJ: 2576–2578. *See also*, DAJ, paras. 270–276 on Grounds of Appeal 19 and 42; DCB (references to Prof. de Jong's evidence throughout the brief).

[256] DCB, para. 540.

[257] TJ: 2578.

confirmed in the Confirmation of Charges, the document which is supposed to provide notice to a defendant of the case being prosecuted against her/him. Thus, the "charged period" serves a specific legal purpose—to provide the temporal framework for the charges. It also defines the legal boundaries of a Trial Chamber's use of evidence in its determination of whether a defendant is guilty beyond a reasonable doubt.

But, in *Ongwen*, the Trial Chamber used the notion of "temporal framework" to essentially create a new legal standard, "linked to the charged period," to determine relevancy of the cultural objections made by the Defence of the Prosecution Experts, Prof. W-P and Dr. GM. In the same sentence in which the Chamber characterized the food request and the absence of a word for "blues" in "many African languages" as "trivial," it also held that these objections [are] "without any serious link to the issue under consideration,"[258] implicitly referring to the "charged period." In effect, the Trial Chamber was imposing "the charged period" temporal standard on cultural factors that directly impacted on (a) how and if people express mental distress and (b) whether Mr. Ongwen's conduct was accurately interpreted, that is, whether he was joking or serious when making a request for termites (white ants [*ngwen*], a Ugandan delicacy).

But the Trial Chamber's use of the "charged period" was selective and inconsistent: it imposed rigid time limits in respect to evidence of mental disease but then ignored these same time limits in respect to possibilities of escape, to reject the duress defence. For example, The Chamber used evidence from 2006, outside the COC's temporal framework, to support its conclusion that escape from the LRA was a "realistic option" for Mr. Ongwen during the "charged period."[259] The Chamber erroneously concluded it was possible for Mr. Ongwen to surrender to the UPDF during the Juba Peace talks in 2006 [outside "the charged period"], but that he refused to do so.[260] This was a significant factor in the Chamber's

[258] TJ: 2463.

[259] TJ: 2581–2672 (conclusions on duress defence, paras. 2635–36 on escape). *See*, DAJ, paras. 558–564 (Grounds 52 and 53); DCB, paras. 28, 671–619, 682, 686, 705–713 (Kony's abuse of spiritualism to prevent abductees from escaping), 714–722 (escape was extremely dangerous due to threat to life of Mr. Ongwen and others), 725.

[260] TJ: 2635–2636.

rejection of the duress defence, holding that Mr. Ongwen was not under threat of death or physical harm.[261] Thus, when it was convenient for the Chamber to go outside the "charged period" and use acts not charged to refute the affirmative defence of duress, and find culpability, it did so.

(7) **Mental health literacy of the Bench**[262]

The Judgment's failure to take into account cultural factors and mental illness also demonstrated that it was not abreast of the key, and very much alive, issue of culture within the profession. This reflects a deficiency in the Trial Chamber's mental health literacy. The mental health literacy of the Judges was restricted (and encumbered) by their racial and cultural biases. The result was that the Chamber took into account only "part of the picture" on the mental health issues. This partial perspective led to its unjustified reliance on factors, like observations of lay witnesses, without understanding the cultural context in which people act (or don't act), and also to its obsession with psychometric testing, particularly for malingering. This is a reminder that mental health literacy among judges cannot be assumed.[263]

---

[261] TJ: 2640.

[262] I am using the term "mental health literacy" to convey a person's understanding of mental health problems, including her/his ability to observe and identify mental health issues. The concept of mental health literacy was first defined by Jorm, et al. "as the knowledge and beliefs about mental illness that contribute to the recognition, management, and prevention of mental illness." *See*, A. F. Jorm , A. E. Korten, P. A. Jacomb, H. Christensen, B. Rodgers, P. Pollitt, "*Mental health literacy" a survey of the public's ability to recognise mental disorders and their beliefs about the effectiveness of treatment,* 166 MED. J. AUST. 182–186 (1997), doi: 10.5694/j.1326-5377.1997.tb140071.x. *Also see* Jue Wu, Lin Zhang, Xu Zhu, Guangrong Jiang, *Mental Health Literacy from the Perspective of Multi-Field Experts in the Context of Chinese Culture*, 18(4) INT. J. ENVIRON. RES. PUBLIC HEALTH (Feb. 2021), 1387, doi: https://doi.org/10.3390/ijerph18041387 (discussing cultural diversity of mental health literacy).

[263] I always thought that professional judges in an international court do not shy away from "deep dives" into medical reports and forensic evidence. I re-thought my assumption after I read a published study of 51 judges and prosecutors in Switzerland which found that when they had questions about medical reports or forensic evidence, the "go to" source was rarely scientific medical literature or databases, and more often was the internet, chiefly Wikipedia or newspapers. Admittedly, the study was based on a small and self-selected sampling for its data collection; therefore, it would obviously be an error to generalize its finding to include all judges. But the study shows that the knowledge of medical issues and scientific literacy skills of legal professionals, including judges, is disparate, at best and can be deficient or lacking. *See*, Carlos Canela, Anna Buadze, Anish Dube, Christian Jackowski, Ingo Pude, Romilda Nellen, Paola Signorin, Michael Liebrenz, "How Do

Part 2: Culture in the *Ongwen* Case

The Role of Spiritualism

In the *Ongwen* case, "spiritual issues occupy the most prominent role in the history of international criminal justice," as Nistor et al. conclude.[264] The role of spiritualism was a key component of Mr. Ongwen's duress defence, where the Defence argued that Kony abused the spiritualism of the Acholi (of which Mr Ongwen is a part) to cement his power and authority over, particularly, new vulnerable child abductees, but also everyone else in the LRA.[265] As the Defence spiritualism expert Prof. Kristof Titeca asked: But to what extent is the ICC equipped to judge a defendant like Ongwen, for whom metaphysical experiences are key to motivations and actions?[266]

In the opening week of its case, the Defence set the cultural stage. It presented evidence of cultural, religious and spiritual practices of the Acholi, through the testimony of religious and cultural leaders. These witnesses included a Cultural Chief of the Pageya clan,[267] and two practicing *ajwakas* (cultural healers).[268] In addition, the Defence later

Legal Experts Cope with Medical Reports and Forensic Evidence? The Experiences, Perceptions and Narratives of Swiss Judges and Other Legal Experts," FRONT. PSYCHIATRY, Vol. 10 (Feb. 2019).

[264] INTERSECTIONS, Adina-Loredana Nistor, Andrew Merrylees and Barbora Holá, "Spellbound at the ICC: the intersection of spirituality and international criminal law," Chapter 8, p. 152. This chapter, based on an analysis of 242 trial transcripts in the *Ongwen* case, focuses on the interactions between international criminal law and culture. Noting the centrality of spiritualism and culture in *Ongwen*, the authors analyze the difficulties of translating and understanding cultural phenomenon, for example, *cen*, for persons in whose own cultural context the concept does not exist. They point out that some expert witnesses, both explicitly and implicitly, referred to Western culture, although this is not defined. They conclude that merging local cultures and the international legal framework "can be painful," and may produce a "cultural Frankenstein" which resembles neither of these two parts, with its own purpose (p. 168).

[265] DCB, paras. 24–30, 477, 617, 692–713.

[266] Titeca, Prof. Kristof, I testified at the trial of one of Joseph Kony's commanders. Here's what the court didn't understand. - The Washington Post, *The Washington Post*, 17 January 2019. Prof. Titeca's testimony is at CR2018_05494.PDF (icc-cpi.int).

[267] TJ: 515.

[268] TJ: 518, 608.

presented an expert on spiritualism and the LRA, Professor Kristof Titeca,[269] as well as the evidence of the Defence Experts, Prof. Ovuga and Dr. Akena, on the impact of culture on mental illness.[270]

But the Trial Chamber explicitly disregarded the cultural evidence: the Cultural Chief's testimony was "too general,"[271] the testimony of the two *ajwakas* was "not directly relevant to the disposal of the charges"[272] and Prof. Titeca's testimony was of "very limited value" because he did not question the veracity of the statements made to him.[273] Prof. Titeca also submitted an Expert Report at trial, entitled "Growing in the Cosmological Space of the LRA."[274] But the Chamber disregarded this Expert Report, as well as his Supplemental Expert Report submitted for sentencing, which focused specifically on the impact of spiritualism on Mr. Ongwen as an individual, because it appeared to have taken statements from Mr. Ongwen at "face value."[275]

One of the Victims' Experts, Dr. Musisi, testified about the relation between Acholi culture and trauma and PTSD. The Trial Chamber "notes" the evidence, but essentially deems it as irrelevant to the case.[276] As to the Defence Experts, I have already detailed the Trial Chamber's wholesale rejection of their evidence, including evidence of how culture impacts on mental illness, and how beliefs in spirit possession can determine a person's judgment of what is considered "normal" behavior. Based

[269] TJ: 596–597.

[270] Discussed *supra.*

[271] TJ: 515.

[272] TJ: 518, 608.

[273] TJ: 596–597.

[274] UGA-D26-0018-3901.

[275] Judgment on Sentence, ICC-02/04-01/15-1819-Red 06-05-2021, CR2021_04230.PDF (icc-cpi.int), para. 114. In addition, the Trial Chamber disregarded Supplemental Expert Reports submitted for sentence from other Defence Experts: Major (ret) Awich on problems of child soldiers returning from war and the UN Standard Minimum Rules for Administration of Juvenile Justice (para. 116); Dr. Erich Awich Ochen on LRA and its early abduction practices (para. 115); Prof. Ovuga on the individual circumstances of Mr. Ongwen for mitigation of sentence based on substantially diminished mental capacity (para. 95).

Also see, Second Public Redacted Version of "Defence request to submit additional evidence.... for determination of sentence," 25 March 2021, paras. 12–31, at CR2021_02561.PDF (icc-cpi.int) and Trial Chamber IX Decision on Additional Evidence, 19 March 2021, at CR2021_02409.PDF (icc-cpi.int).

[276] TJ: 602.

on this, it is hard not to conclude that evidence about culture, and specifically spiritualism, was treated as irrelevant by the *Ongwen* Trial Chamber.

Racial and Cultural Biases and Sentence

The Judgment's outright dismissiveness of culture is especially prominent in the sentencing phase.[277] Rule 145 (1)[278] mandates that a Trial Chamber consider the individual circumstances of the convicted person in determining the sentence. The factors of age, education, social and economic condition are enumerated. The culture and religion of the person are not listed as factors. Rule 145 (2)(a)(i) includes substantially diminished mental capacity[279] and duress as examples of mitigating circumstances.

The Defence placed Mr. Ongwen's Acholi culture front and center as an individual circumstance, and as a factor to be considered for duress as a mitigating circumstance in sentencing. Mr. Ongwen's beliefs in the Spirits and Joseph Kony as a messenger of the Spirits were a lynchpin in the duress argument at sentencing.[280] Starting from the point that "Mr. Ongwen was stolen from his family and his childhood at the age of nine years old and forced to live, grow and work in a rebel cult until his escape on 27 December 2014,"[281] the Defence argued that Mr. Ongwen must undergo all of the appropriate rituals in northern Uganda, including *Mato Oput*.[282] In its Closing Brief, the Defence had requested, as one of

[277] *See*, Demetra Sorvatzioti, *Proportionality and Moral Blameworthiness in Ongwen's ICC Sentencing Decision,* INT. CRIM. LAW REV. 23(5–6) (Brill Nijhoff: 2023), pp. 755–781 ("Sadly, the trial Court's sentencing decision....is not ground-breaking but instead provides a westernised continental narrow view, a mechanical check-list analysis" [p. 781]) at https://doi.org/10.1163/15718123-bja10159.

[278] ICC RPE at Rules-of-Procedure-and-Evidence.pdf (icc-cpi.int).

[279] The Defence argued diminished mental capacity as a mitigating factor, DBS, paras. 85–101; *see also* Judgment on Sentence, paras. 89–105; *Prosecutor v. Ongwen*, ICC-02/04-01/15-1871-Corr-Red2, Second Public Redacted Version of "Corrected Version of 'Defence Document in Support of its Appeal against the Sentencing Decision,' filed on 26 August 2021" (November 16, 2022) ("DAS"), paras. 151–188) at CR2022_06705.PDF (icc-cpi.int); AJ: 195–282.

[280] Public Redacted Version of "Corrected Version of 'Defence Brief on Sentencing,' filed on 1 April 2021," legal-tools.org/doc/c8pnc6/pdf/ ('DBS'), paras. 85–117.

[281] DBS, para. 13.

[282] DBS, para. 39.

its remedies, that if Mr. Ongwen were found guilty, he be placed under the authority of the Acholi traditional justice system to undergo *Mato Oput.*[283] At the sentence phase, the Defence posited that the role of the traditional justice system should be taken into account by the Trial Chamber, in order to assist Mr. Ongwen in his reintegration into Acholi society.[284] On duress caused by Joseph Kony, the Defence described Kony's perversion of Acholi cultural beliefs to control people, including Mr. Ongwen.[285]

In addition, during the sentencing phase, the Defence proposed that Prime Minister Ambrose Olaa of the Ker Kwaro Acholi, the institutional entity charged with Acholi culture in Northern Uganda, testify at the Sentence Hearing on *Mato Oput* and other traditional practices and that his Expert Report be submitted.[286] He was best positioned to explain the Acholi traditional justice system, and the entity he represented, the Ker Kwaro Acholi,[287] which had been instrumental in the passage of Uganda's Amnesty Act, was involved in the peace process with the LRA, and in the re-integration and rehabilitation of ex-LRA abductees into the communities.[288]

The Prosecution did not oppose this request.[289] Nevertheless, the Trial Chamber rejected live testimony from the Prime Minister on traditional justice and mechanisms of reconciliation and restorative justice in Acholi culture in Northern Uganda.[290] The reasoning appears to be based on the

[283] DCB, para. 733; Sentence Judgment, paras. 17–43 (Trial Chamber's rejection of evidence of traditional justice mechanisms).

[284] DBS, paras. 52–54.

[285] DBS, paras. 102–117; *see also,* DCB, paras. 675–730; DAS, paras. 192–204; DAJ, paras. 5, 307–319, 499–544, 558–563, 576–603, 611–615 (on duress and spiritualism).

[286] Second Public Redacted Version of "Defence request to submit additional evidence for Trial Chamber IX's determination of the sentence," filed 26 February 2021, 25 March 2021, paras. 25–27, CR2021_02561.PDF (icc-cpi.int); *see also* DAS, paras. 100–111 at CR2022_06705.PDF (icc-cpi.int).

[287] Ker Kwaro Acholi - The Official Website of the Paramount Chiefdom of Acholi.

[288] DBS, paras. 27–36.

[289] Prosecution Response, para. 8 at CR2021_01974.PDF (icc-cpi.int).

[290] Decision on "Defence request to submit additional evidence for Trial Chamber IX's determination of the sentence," para. 20 at CR2021_02409.PDF (icc-cpi.int).

scope of the proposed testimony and a determination that it was unnecessary, given that his documentary evidence had been submitted.[291]

The Trial Chamber's rejection, alone, of live testimony from the Prime Minister raises questions about its stance on culture. But, when considered in the context of the Chamber's conclusion in its Judgment on Sentence, 6 May 2021, that it decided not to consider the submissions and evidence on the "Acholi Traditional Justice System,"[292] its reasoning shouts volumes about cultural bias and its impact on jurisprudence.

The Trial Chamber gives a number of reasons. The first two are based on the law: (#1) traditional justice mechanisms are not found in the Rome Statute, and its "legal hands" are tied by Article 23 (*nulla poena sine lege*); (#2) the Chamber gives deference to a ruling from the High Court of Uganda that traditional justice should not supplant formal justice.[293] The Chamber, however, offers no perspective on if, and how, the ICC should integrate traditional justice practices and systems under the rubric of complementarity (which has been implemented at the ICC solely in terms of investigation and prosecution, but not in sentencing).

The third reason (#3) criticizes the Defence for its "abstract" request,[294] and for not providing a "comprehensive definition" of traditional justice mechanisms.[295] Yet, the same Trial Chamber, when presented with an opportunity to hear the live testimony from the Ker Kwaro Acholi Prime Minister, rejected the Defence request. In the fourth reason (#4), the Trial Chamber explains that if it were to consider the Acholi traditional justice system, then victims who were not Acholi would be excluded.[296] This explanation conveniently ignores that Mr. Ongwen, the defendant, who is also a victim, is an Acholi, and that it is he who has to reconcile with the community and be re-integrated and rehabilitated. The

[291] The same reasoning was used by the Trial Chamber to reject live testimony from the child soldier Expert, Major (ret) Pollar Awich and from Expert Prof. Eric Awich Ochen, both of whom had previously testified at trial.

[292] Judgment on Sentence ('Sentence Judgment'), ICC-02/04-01/15-1819-Red 06-05-2021, CR2021_04230.PDF (icc-cpi.int), para. 43. *See* Trial Chamber's reasoning at paras. 15–43.

[293] Sentence Judgment, para. 34.

[294] *Ibid.*, para. 34.

[295] *Ibid.*, paras. 28–29.

[296] *Ibid.*, para. 30.

Chamber's fifth reason (#5) is that some of the victims, but particularly two experts, presented evidence that they were skeptical of the *Mato Oput* process and traditional justice mechanisms.[297] Neither expert is Acholi (one is European and the other is Ugandan, who is not Acholi). Here, the Chamber is making a judgment about traditional justice and whose interests it represents – although the Judges have no standing as members of the cultural and religious communities in Northern Uganda.

Racial and Cultural Biases Overlap in Sentencing

How the Trial Chamber's racial and cultural biases operate together is best illustrated in its final reason for discounting evidence at sentencing about the Acholi traditional justice mechanism. In the sixth reason (#6), the Chamber notes that a showing of remorse is a predicate for a traditional justice mechanism; the Chamber then places the blame for its rejection of the traditional justice mechanism evidence on Mr. Ongwen, because he did not show remorse.[298]

This is a misrepresentation of the record: at the Sentence Hearing a few weeks before its decision, Mr. Ongwen addressed the Chamber and explicitly expressed remorse – as a human being - for what happened to households in Northern Uganda, including his own family because of the LRA. Mr. Ongwen's parents were brutally killed and his siblings are not "mentally okay," even up until the present. He asked forgiveness for the people that he was ordered to kill.[299]

The Trial Chamber did not accept Mr. Ongwen's statements as "genuine remorse" and characterized them as "self-pity," and that he was claiming that his suffering as a victim was equal to the other victims in the case.[300] Here, the "Ongwen Exception," again, reared its racist head: functioning as a blindspot, it blocked the Chamber from hearing and interpreting what Mr. Ongwen, a Black Acholi defendant, said about

[297] *Ibid.*, paras. 32–41.

[298] *Ibid.*, para. 42.

[299] Sentence Hearing Transcript T-261, CR2021_03573.PDF (icc-cpi.int), pp. 21–22. *See also*, p. 26, ll. 4–13.

[300] Sentence Judgment, para. 42.

forgiveness and his remorse. But, the bottom line is that the Chamber did not regard the defendant, Mr. Ongwen, as a human being, and treated him as if he were invisible. Taken together with the Chamber's overt rejection of any evidence at trial or sentence of Mr. Ongwen's cultural and spiritual identity as a Black, Acholi man, this illustrates that the judicial cultural and racial biases envelope each other and produce racist and culturist jurisprudence.

Culture in ICC Judgments Before *Ongwen*

While *Ongwen* demonstrates Trial Chamber IX's rejection of cultural factors in its Judgment and Sentence and its negation of the importance of race, it would be wrong to conclude that all Trial Chambers at the ICC have totally ignored issues of culture in their judgments. This is not the case. But, how different Trial Chambers understand cultural factors, or even whether they acknowledge them, affects their judgments and sentencing in their courtrooms.

In *Katanga* (2014), Trial Chamber II sought the assistance of a sociologist to understand the cultural context of the conflict in Bogoro, Democratic Republic of the Congo.[301] In fact, the Chamber took an activist approach, questioning almost half the witnesses, including the defendant, about socio-cultural aspects.[302] In its Judgment, the Chamber criticized the Prosecution for not presenting the socio-cultural aspects of its evidence, which was necessary for an interpretation of the evidence: for example, the significance of local customs and the role of family relationships in Ituri, and the role of fetish-priests (*féticheurs*), who were also directly concerned with military matters.[303] The Sentence Judgment[304] does not specifically discuss cultural factors, but the Trial Chamber

[301] INTERSECTIONS, Adina-Loredana Nistor, Andrew Merrylees and Barbora Holá, Chapter 8, p. 151, n. 30.

[302] INTERSECTIONS, Suzanne Schot, Chapter 9, p. 177.

[303] *Katanga* Judgment, legal-tools.org/doc/f74b4f/pdf/, paras. 66, 67, 1254, 1258.

[304] *Katanga* Sentence Judgment, CR2015_18046.PDF (icc-cpi.int).

accepted Mr. Germain Katanga's positive role in disarming and demobilizing child soldiers in Ituri as a mitigating factor.[305]

In *Bemba* (2016), Trial Chamber III convicted Mr. Bemba, as a leader of the Movement for the Liberation of the Congo (MLC), a militia group, based on command responsibility. Yet, the Chamber's understanding of the MLC was centered on structures of Western conventional armies, and ignored the cultural influences on authority in militia and rebel groups in Africa.[306] In 2018, the Appeals Chamber overturned the Trial Chamber's decision and acquitted Mr. Bemba, who has returned to the Democratic Republic of Congo.

Al Mahdi [307] (2016) was the first case in which a Trial Chamber (TC VIII) opined on the war crime of destruction of religious and historic monuments in its Judgment.[308] Mr. Al Mahdi, a religious leader and appointed head of "*Hisbah,*" a morality brigade, pled guilty, as a co-perpetrator, to intentionally directing the attacks on ten historic and religious monuments in Timbuktu, Mali in 2012. All but one of these monuments had been designated as UNESCO world heritage sites.[309] The Chamber addressed the definition of cultural heritage and recognized it in its findings on the "significant" gravity of the crime.[310] However, it failed to recognize the impact of culture – in this case, religion – on the defendant. The Chamber did not consider Mr. Al Mahdi's religion as an individual circumstance under Rule 145,[311] although it noted that the crime was committed for religious motives.[312] Thus, Mr. Al Mahdi's individual culture, like Mr. Ongwen's, was explicitly disregarded as an individual circumstance relevant to sentence, under Rule 145. The Chamber, did, however, consider Mr. Al Mahdi's initial reluctance to destroy the

[305] *Katanga* Sentence Judgment, para. 115.

[306] INTERSECTIONS, Ingrid Roestenburg-Morgan, Chapter 16, p. 332. She also points out that the failure to "accommodate" cultural context can "compromise and undermine fairness" in the proceedings (p. 333).

[307] *Al Mahdi* Judgment and Sentence, CR2016_07244.PDF (icc-cpi.int).

[308] Rome Statute, Article 8(2)(e)(iv).

[309] *See Al Mahdi* plea agreement and facts at CR2016_06550.PDF (icc-cpi.int).

[310] *Al Mahdi* Judgment and Sentence, para. 82.

[311] *Ibid.*, para. 96.

[312] *Ibid.*, para. 81.

sites, and his recommendation not to use a bulldozer as mitigating circumstances.[313]

How Can the ICC Move Forward on Culture and Race After *Ongwen*?

The *Ongwen* case illustrates that (1) there is no mandate for racial or cultural factors to be considered by a Trial Chamber; (2) there is no uniformity as to whether each Trial Chamber addresses cultural issues, and, if they do, how;[314] (3) culture should be interpreted broadly, and it is not one-dimensional and separate from everything else, but integrated into all aspects of the case, including the defences excluding criminal responsibility under Article 31;[315] (4) complementarity has to include traditional justice mechanisms, especially in sentencing; (5) culture, race and disability are factors of an individual's circumstances, and should be explicitly included in Rule 145; and (6) the issue of legal standards to be applied to guilt, versus legal standards to be applied to access to justice for mentally disabled persons, can be confused and conflated by the Trial Chamber.[316]

The *Ongwen* case is distinguished by the Trial Chamber's outright rejection of *any* relevance of cultural evidence in its Judgment and Sentence, and its use of a racist construct, the "Ongwen Exception," to justify its legal conclusions. Hence, the *Ongwen* Judgment's "legitimacy" score is at zero, or in the minus numbers. *Ongwen*, as a legal barometer, indicates that the ICC's jurisprudence and practice on race and culture is moving backwards, and very quickly. The question is: can the ICC reverse this trend? If so, what is needed for forward motion?

---

[313] *Al Mahdi* Judgment and Sentence, paras. 89–93.

[314] The divergent approaches to cultural issues of the *Ongwen* and *Al Hassan* Trial Chambers, discussed *supra.*, illustrate this point. In addition, the inconsistencies in expert evidence given by the same experts - Prof. W-P and Dr. GM - on the same issues in different cases, in *Ongwen* and *Al Hassan*, demonstrate that some Trial Chambers accept inconsistent evidence as reliable and credible.

[315] *See*, INTERSECTIONS, Higgins, Chapter 12, p. 248 (proposal that defendant's cultural context be raised within defences in Rome Statute, Articles 31–33); Roestenburg-Morgan, Chapter 16.

[316] *See* Chap. 2.

(1) **As a prerequisite, the ICC has to identify, assess and evaluate the extent of the problem of racial and cultural biases in its judgments, starting from its beginnings.** This potentially could lead to a revision of judgments, if these biases were operating in a significant manner to affect the outcome of the judgment. Article 84 (revision of conviction or sentence) of the Rome Statute makes no explicit provisions for revision of conviction or sentence based on bias; it identifies grounds for revision as newly discovered evidence, use of false or forged evidence and serious misconduct or breach of duty of judges.[317] However, racial and cultural bias, as in the case of *Ongwen*, resulted in wrongful convictions which violate internationally recognized human rights. Therefore, as per Rome Statute, Article 21(3), an argument could be constructed for revision based on the Court's "interests of justice" jurisdiction.

(2) **The Trial Chamber should use its own racial and cultural experts** (in addition to the experts presented by the parties), as the *Katanga* Trial Chamber did, to assist the judges in interpreting evidence in its racial and cultural context.[318]

(3) **Rule 145 (determination of sentence) should be amended to include the factors of race, culture, religion and disability[319] as individual circumstances.** Rome Statute, Article 78(1) mandates that a Trial Chamber consider the individual circumstances of the convicted person in determining the sentence. Rule 145 (1) (c) enumerates the factors of age, education, social and economic condition of the convicted person, in addition to factors related to involvement in the crime and harm caused to victims and their families. The explicit inclusion of race, culture, religion and disability would situate these factors within the structural framework of the Rome Statute

---

[317] Rome Statute, Article 84(1).

[318] *See*, Gregor Maučec, INTERSECTIONS, Chapter 10 (judicial cultural competence essential for judges to carry out their responsibilities in a fair and just manner and advocates an activist approach for judges to familiarize themselves with the cultures involved in a case, including using cultural experts appointed by the Court).

[319] *See* Chap. 2.

in which the ICC operates. Michelle Coleman points out that the Statute already gives wide discretion to the Trial Chamber to include cultural factors, if it chooses, not only in determinations of gravity of the crime, but in assessing aggravating and mitigating circumstances.[320] But, given the lack of uniformity in each Trial Chamber's approach, the explicit inclusion of race, culture, religion and disability as additional factors means that a Trial Chamber would be mandated to consider these factors "up front" in its determination of sentence.

(4) **The Rome Statute, Article 78 and its implementation Rule 145 (determination of sentence) should be amended to include traditional justice mechanisms within its process.** The principle of complementarity, found in the Rome Statute's Preamble, has been applied in investigation and prosecution phases, but not to the sentencing phase. Its relevance, especially in the re-integration and rehabilitation of a convicted person into the community from which s/he hails,[321] should be recognized through its explicit inclusion in sentencing. This would avoid a repetition of the situation in *Ongwen*, where the Defence offers the Trial Chamber an opportunity for complementarity with the traditional justice mechanisms, but the Chamber rejects it.

It would be naïve to expect that the implementation of these suggestions is enough to reverse the ICC's course, or that it would have a "spill-over" effect on the ICC's jurisprudence. But, this provides a start, which is sorely needed if the ICC is going to be seen – through its actions - as a forum for international justice, applying the rule of law to all, and promoting fairness and inclusiveness in its practices in the courtroom, as well as in its jurisprudence.

---

[320] Michelle Coleman, INTERSECTIONS, Chapter 14.

[321] *See*, DBS, paras. 40–55.

Conclusion

Culture and race have always mattered, including (and especially) in courts of law. But the *Ongwen* Judgment stands for the opposite: it says, "culture and race do not matter." As this chapter has explored, the Trial Chamber's racial and cultural biases negatively impacted on its assessment of the Defence Experts' evidence and resulted in its rejection of the Article 31 defences. In addition, the Trial Chamber's refusal at the sentencing phase to consider the Acholi traditional justice system and hear live testimony from the Prime Minister of the Ker Kwaro Acholi, indicates a rejection of complementarity with traditional justice mechanisms in sentencing. It also demonstrates the Chamber's indifference to the effects of spiritualism, as well as the LRA's culture of child soldiering, on Mr. Ongwen.

While the *Ongwen* Judgment obviously impacts Mr. Ongwen, it is also a warning bell to all persons with mental illness and to all child soldiers who may be prosecuted at the ICC in future proceedings. The *Ongwen* case demonstrates that mental incapacity and criminal coercive circumstances (in cults like the LRA, militias or other military entities) of these potential defendants will not be fairly assessed. Unfortunately, the Judgment in *Ongwen* is a a handbook of what goes wrong when race, culture and mental illness are not affirmatively considered in the ICC's jurisprudence.

The ICC needs to do better in order to earn its legitimacy and be worthy of respect from both defendants and victims who have high stakes in its proceedings. This starts with applying the rule of law to all, and ensuring fairness in its proceedings. But it also means confronting its racial and cultural biases within its structure, as well as within the decisions and judgments which it renders.

The ICC should not squander the opportunity which the recognition of the *Ongwen* Judgment's errors provides: to become a judicial institution whose legitimacy is founded on fairness, inclusivity and a respect for human rights. Whether the ICC will succeed and ensure that race and culture matter in its jurisprudence is key. This will determine the ICC's relevance and its very existence within the international justice regime.

2

Getting Disability and Reasonable Accommodation Right: What Went Wrong in the *Ongwen* Case and the Need for a Presumption of Mental Disability for Defendants

Abstract Mr. Dominic Ongwen ("Mr. Ongwen") is the first ICC defendant to assert an affirmative defence, under Article 31, for exclusion of criminal responsibility, based on mental disease or defect and on duress. This was a complete defence against the 70 charges and seven modes of liability confirmed against him in the Confirmation of Charges ("COC") decision. In February 2021, the Trial Chamber ("Chamber" or "Court") convicted Mr. Ongwen of 61 counts and two modes of liability and sentenced him to 25 years' imprisonment in May 2021. In December 2022, the Appeals Chamber affirmed the Trial Judgment and Sentence.

The *Ongwen* case illustrates the lacunae in the ICC's implementation of its obligation to reasonably accommodate mentally disabled

---

Special thanks and appreciation to the *Ongwen* Defence Experts, Professor Emilio Ovuga and Dr. Dickens Akena for generously sharing their knowledge with the *Ongwen* Defence team and raising our awareness about mental health and mental illness. Also, thanks to Chief Charles A. Taku, Tibor Bajnovič, Amirah Mimano and Cheryl P. Williams for their invaluable assistance.
The author has a personal interest in reasonable accommodation for disabilities. She was disabled as a result of an auto accident in 1989, and settled a lawsuit against her employer, The Legal Aid Society (New York City), under the Americans with Disabilities (ADA) Act, for failing to provide reasonable accommodation. *See Lyons v. Legal Aid Society*, 68 F.3d 1512 (2d Cir. 1995) (reasonable accommodation includes access to the workplace, as well as access within the workplace).

B. S. Lyons, *Race, Culture and Mental Illness in the International Criminal Court's Ongwen Judgment: Biases and Blindspots*, https://doi.org/10.1007/978-3-031-73683-4_2

defendants and to provide them with equal access to justice. I posit that the Trial Chamber was obstructed by a mental disability blindspot, which resulted in the denial of Mr. Ongwen's fair trial rights. To remedy this problem, I propose that the ICC make available to a defendant, if s/he should choose to invoke it, a presumption of mental disability, based on the reality that the mass trauma in the ICC "situations" does not discriminate in its victims.

Keywords Mental disability • Reasonable accommodation • Mental disability blindspot • Access to justice • Convention on the Rights of Persons with Disabilities ("CRPD") • Presumption of mental disability • ICC

Introduction

Dominic Ongwen was abducted in 1987 by the Lord's Resistance Army ("LRA") in northern Uganda when he was eight or nine years old and trafficked as a child soldier. He made multiple unsuccessful attempts to escape, and finally succeeded in late 2014. Mr. Ongwen turned himself into the International Criminal Court ("ICC") in 2015. Mr. Ongwen's defence was that he was not responsible for the crimes of the LRA, based on his mental illnesses and duress, stemming from his abduction and subsequent coercion and indoctrination under Joseph Kony within the LRA.

Dominic Ongwen was, and is, mentally ill. He is also mentally disabled, which requires reasonable accommodations from the Court to provide him equal access to justice. No doubt, his diagnosed mental illnesses also contribute to his mental disability. But, throughout the case, it was an uphill battle (which the Defence, most often, lost) to convince the Trial Chamber to recognize and reasonably accommodate his disability, despite its legal obligation to do so. The Chamber conflated mental disability with mental illness, and did not apply the appropriate legal standards for each.

I posit that the reason is the Trial Chamber simply did not view Mr. Ongwen as mentally disabled. It had a "mental disability" blindspot which obstructed it from seeing Mr. Ongwen's disability and, hence, from reasonably and effectively accommodating it. Where a Court fails to reasonably and effectively accommodate a mentally disabled defendant, it violates the fundamental principle that mental health is a human right.

The implementation of a defendant's fair trial rights is circumscribed by, and must take account of, mental disability. The Trial Chamber's violation of Mr. Ongwen's right to decide whether or not to testify in his own defence by denying the Defence request for a medical examination is an example of the Trial Chamber's mental disability blindspot. It prevented the Chamber from implementing the principle of equality which applies to all persons before it, including mentally disabled defendants.

To address this problem, I argue that the ICC should make available a presumption of mental disability for defendants in its cases.[1] The choice of whether or not to invoke this presumption is up to the defendant alone; it is not a presumption which the Court can impose on a defendant. The Court's obligation is simply to make it available. This judicial recognition of disability would automatically trigger the legal obligation for reasonable accommodation, which is essential to promote equal access to justice for the mentally disabled defendant.

This presumption has three points:

(a) The presumption is based on the recognized mass trauma of conflict situations, which comprise the Court's docket, and the indiscriminate effects of this trauma on people in the conflict areas. The ICC already implements procedures and safeguards for traumatized victims or witnesses and for vulnerable groups.[2] A vulnerable witness may be provided with a support person in court or perhaps other services through the Registry's Victims and Witnesses Unit at the ICC.[3] The problem is that these measures for protection of traumatized witnesses do not automatically apply to defendants who may also be traumatized and re-traumatized during the proceedings.

---

[1] This chapter is focused on the ICC. However, a presumption of mental disability is applicable to any court or tribunal which deals with cases arising out of conflict and war.

[2] *See* Rome Statute, Art. 68(1) and RPE, Rule 87.

[3] *See* The Trauma Expert | International Criminal Court (icc-cpi.int) (describing work of ICC Trauma Expert with the Victims and Witnesses Unit).

(b) A presumption of mental disability is based on a minimal standard, a *prima facie* showing. It is not based on the higher standard of proof beyond a reasonable doubt which is applied to determine guilt, for example, when affirmative defences under Article 31 are asserted by the Defence.
(c) The presumption is invoked, solely at the discretion of the Defence, who is most often the "first responder" to its client's mental disability and mental illness. It cannot be imposed by the Court on defendants. However, the Court's onus is to decide measures which reasonably accommodate the disability and guarantee equal access to justice in compliance with international law.

Unfortunately, the Trial Chamber's holdings in the *Ongwen* case on mental illness and reasonable accommodation for mental disability are examples of "bad law and bad practice." But, their implications help to focus on how disability is treated in the ICC's Rome Statute ("Statute"), and the need for ICC compliance with recognized international human rights law, as per Article 21(3).

Part 1: The Legal Framework

Mental Health as a Human Right Provides the Context for Reasonable Accommodation

International human rights instruments protect the right to health, which includes mental health and the rights of persons with disabilities, including mental disabilities.[4] Therefore, the concept of mental health as a

[4] *See* Carla A. Arena Ventura, *International Law, Mental Health and Human Rights*, Center for Civil and Human Rights, University of Notre Dame, June 2014. This article includes Table 1, listing International and Inter-American Human Rights instruments. *See also* Comfort Asanbe, Ayorkor Gaba, and J. Yang, *Mental Health is a Human Right*, PSYCHOLOGY INTERNATIONAL, December 2018, American Psychological Association (discussing mental health's importance in the Universal Declaration of Human Rights and the adoption of a right to health framework for 2030 Sustainable Development Goals [SDG] where Target 3.4 addresses prevention and treatment, and promotes mental health and well-being).

human right provides the framework for a presumption of, and reasonable accommodation for, mental disability.

More than 15 years prior to the entering into force of the Convention on the Rights of Persons with Disabilities ("CRPD"),[5] the UN General Assembly adopted the Principles for the Protection of Persons with Mental Illness and the Improvement of Mental Health Care ("Principles"), in 1991.[6] These Principles provide the basis for protection of persons with mental illness and improvement of mental health treatment. Principle 1 states that "all persons have the right to the best mental health care, which shall be part of the health and social system."[7]

The broad, inclusive wording of Principle 1 is significant: "all persons" means everyone has the right to mental health care. This is emphasized in its definition of "mental health care" which "includes analysis and diagnosis of a person's mental condition, and treatment, care and rehabilitation for a mental illness or *suspected mental illness*"[8] (italics added). Hence, a person, to be protected under the Principles, does not have to have a "declared" or "proven" mental illness to enjoy the right to the "best available mental health care." If a mental illness is even suspected, that is sufficient. This indicates an approach which recognizes that mental health is not static, and narrowly defined—but exists on a spectrum. So, a mentally disabled person, who may be suffering from a mental disability but not a full-fledged mental illness at the time of an examination, is within the protected and entitled category. The right to reasonable accommodation for mental disability would fall within this context.

The CRPD defines discrimination on the basis of disability as including "all forms of discrimination, *including denial of reasonable*

---

[5] The CRPD and Optional Protocol were adopted 31 December 2006 by UNGA Resolution A/RES/61/106 and entered into force 3 May 2008. As of 25 June 2023, there were 164 signatories and 187 States Parties. Available at A/RES/61/106: Convention on the rights of persons with disabilities (un.org). The CRPD is identified as a core international human rights instrument by the Office of the High Commissioner on Human Rights (OHCHR) at The Core International Human Rights Instruments and their monitoring bodies | OHCHR. In 2014, the Human Rights Council appointed its first Special Rapporteur on the Rights of Persons with Disabilities.

[6] UNGA Res. 46/119, 17 December 1991, available at The protection of persons with mental illness and the improvement of mental health care : (un.org).

[7] Principles, para. 1.

[8] Principles, Definitions.

accommodation"[9] (emphasis added). The equality and non-discrimination of persons with disabilities is found in CRPD, Article 5. CRPD, Article 12 addresses the right of persons with disability to equal recognition before the law, including "appropriate measures to provide access … to the support they may require in exercising their legal capacity."[10] CRPD, Article 13 states the right to access to justice, and specifies that effective access includes "procedural and age-appropriate accommodations" to ensure equal access to justice.[11]

The language of the Convention confers obligations on States Parties, and includes a continuing reporting mechanism to the Committee on the Rights of Persons with Disabilities.[12] However, its basic principles are applicable to the ICC under the Rome Statute's framework in Article 21(3), which is the anti-discrimination clause in the Statute. It mandates that the ICC apply and interpret the law consistent with internationally recognized human rights, and in a non-discriminatory manner. However, the ICC Statute is silent on disability: it is not an enumerated category of discrimination in Article 21(3), but is relegated to "other status." Nor are crimes based on disability specified in Articles 7 (crimes against humanity)[13] and 8 (war crimes).

Disability should be named. This would be consistent with the status of the CRPD as a human rights treaty and would give disability a legal and practical visibility. The Assembly of States Parties needs to amend the Rome Statute, Article 21(3) to include disability, so that there is no ambiguity that the ICC protects the right to equality for persons with disabilities and applies non-discrimination on the grounds of disability in its practices.

---

[9] CRPD, Art. 2. In addition, the core principles of equality, non-discrimination and accessibility are among those embodied in General Principles (Article 3), and reflected in obligations of States Parties in General Obligations (Article 4).

[10] *Ibid.*, Art.12, §§ 1, 2, 3.

[11] *Ibid.*, Art. 13, § 1.

[12] *Ibid.*, Art. 33, 34, 35, 36, 37.

[13] *See* William I. Pons, Janet E. Lord, and Michael Ashley Stein, *Disability, Human Rights Violations, and Crimes Against Humanity*, AJIL, Cambridge University Press: August 2021. *See also* Janet Lord, Rosemary Kayess, William Pons, and Michael Ashley Stein, *The U.N. Process for a Crimes Against Humanity Treaty Has Finally Started. Will It Account for Persons with Disabilities?* 26 May 2023 at https://www.justsecurity.org/86724 (last visited 28 September 2023).

Reasonable Accommodation for Mental Disability Is a Fair Trial Right

UN General Assembly Resolution 46/119 includes twenty-five Principles for the Protection of Persons with Mental Illness and for the Improvement of Mental Health Care.[14] These include the right to "exercise all civil, political, economic, social and cultural rights,"[15] as recognized in a number of human rights instruments which also embody the right to a fair trial. Thus, the Principles affirm the idea that a denial of the right of reasonable accommodation for a mentally disabled client is also a violation of her/his fair trial right.

Further, the Principles emphasize that these fundamental freedoms and rights are applicable to criminal offenders.[16] Principle 20 reinforces the right of criminal offenders to "receive the best available mental health care ... to the fullest extent possible, with only such limited modifications and exceptions as are necessary in the circumstances. *No such modifications and exceptions shall prejudice the person's rights under the instruments noted in paragraph 5 of Principle 1*"[17] (emphasis added). The instruments in Principle 1, § 5 are the UDHR, the ICESCR, the ICCPR, the Declaration on the Rights of Disabled Persons and the Body of Principles for the Protection of All Persons under Any Form of Detention or Imprisonment.

The Rome Statute, Article 67, enumerates the rights of the defendant before the International Criminal Court. It contains an anti-discrimination clause[18] which is fundamental to the exercise of these rights. The first sentence states that

> In the determination of any charge, the accused shall be entitled to a public hearing, having regard to the provisions of this Statute, to a fair hearing

[14] UNGA Res. 46/119, adopted 17 December 1991, Annex.

[15] *Ibid.*, Principle 1, § 5.

[16] *Ibid.*, Principle 20.

[17] *Ibid.*, Principle 20, § 2.

[18] William A. Schabas and Yvonne McDermott, Article 67, Section 18, pp. 1659–1660 in Otto Triffterer and Kai Ambos (eds), THE ROME STATUTE OF THE INTERNATIONAL CRIMINAL COURT, A COMMENTARY, 3rd edn. (C.H. Beck-Hart-Nomos 2015).

> conducted impartially, and to the following minimum guarantees, *in full equality*. (Emphasis added)

Thus, from the outset, it is clear that these rights must be implemented in a non-discriminatory manner. The right remains the same—whether a defendant is disabled or not disabled. But for a disabled defendant, her/his disability impacts on the ability to exercise all of the fair trial rights under Article 67.

The issue of reasonable accommodation of a mental disability, or any other disability, to enable a disabled person to exercise her/his rights in the judicial process, is not a revolutionary notion. It is embodied in principles of the right to access to justice and reasonable accommodation found in international instruments. But the ICC's full compliance with these principles is long overdue, especially where requests for reasonable accommodation impact on a defendant's exercise of her/his fair trial rights.

Who Is Responsible for the Mental Health of the Defendant?

There is enough responsibility for the mental health of a defendant to be shared amongst many parties and institutions, including the courts and detention centres, involved in a criminal proceeding. But the initial and principal responsibility has been assigned in the international courts and tribunals to defence counsel. The defence counsel is the "first responder." And, depending on the level of awareness and responsiveness of the court, the defence counsel may also be "responder in chief" and may be—in some situations—the "sole responder."

At the ICTR, references to clients with disability are found in the Code of Professional Conduct for Defence Counsel. This Code places the initial duty on a defence counsel to identify a client's disability, and inform the Court; and to take whatever steps are necessary to legally represent the client.[19] Similar provisions are found at the ICTY in its Code

[19] ICTR Code of Professional Conduct for Defence Counsel (2008), Art. 10.

of Professional Conduct for Counsel at Article 16.[20] At the ICC, Article 9 of the Code of Professional Conduct for Counsel, which applies to defence counsel, places the onus on defence counsel, but—unlike the *ad hoc* tribunals—includes language prohibiting inequality, based on numerous grounds, including disability.[21]

From a strictly legal perspective, this makes sense: it is the defence counsel who represents a mentally disabled defendant, and has a privileged relationship with her/his client. The Office of the Prosecutor ("OTP"), which is prosecuting the defendant, has no independent access to her/him, but it is accountable for ensuring that its conduct in the proceedings is fair and non-discriminatory toward the defendant. The ICC's Code of Conduct for the Office of the Prosecutor (OTP)[22] includes respect for human rights and the fundamental principle of equality before the law,[23] and mandates "honorable conduct" which includes "dignified, courteous and sensitive conduct towards all victims and witnesses, in particular children, elderly people, persons with disabilities and victims of sexual and gender violence ..."[24] and promotes equal treatment and non-discrimination and non-harassment of colleagues based on, among other factors, disability.[25]

Although defence counsel are expected to play a pivotal role vis-à-vis a mentally disabled defendant, make no mistake: the decision-making power never leaves the Judges, who determine critical issues for a mentally disabled defendant. These can include, for example (a) deciding whether the defendant is competent to participate in the trial; (b) ordering expert examinations; (c) deciding whether and what reasonable accommodations are required for the defendant's participation in the proceedings; (d) ruling on requests from counsel related to a defendant's mental health status and fair trial rights; (e) overseeing the implementation of any directives by the Detention Centre; etc.

[20] ICTY Code of Professional Conduct for Counsel Appearing before the International Tribunal (2009), Art. 16.

[21] ICC Code of Professional Conduct for Counsel (2011) Art. 9, §§ 1, 2.

[22] Code of Conduct for the Office of the Prosecutor, 5 September 2013.

[23] *Ibid.*, Introduction (4).

[24] *Ibid.*, Chapter 2, § 3, para. 26 (d).

[25] *Ibid.*, Chapter 4, § 1, paras. 58, 59.

Judicial decision-making power does not make a Trial Chamber the arbitrator of mental disability and mental illness. But the Chamber, under law, has the responsibility to reasonably accommodate a defendant's disability.[26] This means that accommodation of a defendant's mental disability needs to be added to its checklist of fair trial procedures. This is a step to level the playing field, and to ensure the mentally disabled defendant's fair trial rights.

Part 2: The *Ongwen* Case—The Fight to Close the Accommodation Gap

At the time of the *Ongwen* case, no ICC Trial Chamber, on its own initiative (without Defence requests), had assessed that mental disability may be a factor preventing the defendant's meaningful participation[27] in the proceedings, and suggested potential reasonable accommodations to a defendant. If this had been done, it would mean that the ICC recognizes that mental disability impacts the exercise of a defendant's fair trial rights.

In the *Ongwen* case, the Defence litigated over a period of years for various reasonable accommodations for Mr. Ongwen's mental disability, starting in 2015 with a request for breaks from the Pre-Trial Chamber, during the "Article 56" proceedings.[28] In 2018 and 2019, following the recommendations of the Detention Center, the Defence made repeated requests to the Trial Chamber to adopt a four-day trial schedule, with Wednesdays "off," to accommodate Mr. Ongwen's treatment schedule for his mental illnesses at the Detention Centre.[29] But extensive Defence

[26] Although this paper refers mainly to the Trial Chamber, the obligation to accommodate a disabled defendant applies to all Chambers in the judicial process.

[27] "Meaningful participation" means that a defendant can exercise his or her fair trial rights. Judgment, *Strugar*, ICTY, No. IT -01-42-A, Appeals Chamber, 17 July 2008, para. 55; Decision on the fitness of Laurent Gbagbo to take part in the proceedings before this Court, *Gbagbo* (ICC-02/11-01/11-286-Red), Trial Chamber, 2 November 2012, para. 50.

[28] DCB, para. 123.

[29] *See* DCB, paras. 120–146; DAJ, paras. 247–250.

litigation—spanning many months—was required for the four-day "sitting schedule" to be implemented.[30]

These examples of reasonable accommodations, which are determined by the specifics of the disability, are essential to the exercise of fair trial rights. Without reasonable accommodations, the fair trial rights cannot be realized. But logistical accommodations were not the only reasonable accommodations required for Mr. Ongwen. One of the most egregious failures of the Trial Chamber to reasonably accommodate Mr. Ongwen's mental disability resulted in denying him the right to decide whether he wanted to testify or not, pursuant to its obligations to conduct a fair trial and the right of a defendant to present a defence.[31]

The right to testify (or not) is one of the most important rights in presenting a defence.[32] In *Ongwen,* the Defence requested, under Rule 135, an impartial psychiatric examination of Mr. Ongwen,[33] in order to "make a diagnosis as to any mental condition or disorder that Mr. Ongwen may suffer at the present time that makes him unable to make an informed decision whether or not to testify in his defence."[34] The Trial Chamber denied the Defence request.[35] Ruling on the Defence Request to appeal its decision, the Chamber held that "the question of whether the accused may be mentally disabled was never considered in the Impugned

---

[30] DCB, paras. 136–145.

[31] Rome Statute, Art. 64 (2) and Art. 67(1)(e).

[32] *See* Marjorie L. Rifkin, *The Criminal Defendant's Right to Testify: The Right to Be Seen but Not Heard,* 21 COLUM. HUM. RTS. L. REV. 253 (1989) (right to testify derived from U.S. Constitution and is fundamental to ensure a fair trial).

[33] RPE, Rule 135.

[34] Defence Urgent Request to Order a Medical Examination of Mr. Ongwen, *Ongwen* (ICC-02/04-01/15-1595-Red), Defence, 16 September 2019, § 3.

[35] The Defence filed three Rule 135 requests, and all were denied by the Trial Chamber. The 1st request (ICC-02/04-01/15-620-Red) was made prior to the opening of the trial, 5 December 2016; Decision (ICC-02/04-01/15-637-Red), 16 December 2016. The 2nd request (ICC-02/04-01/15-1405-Red2) was filed on 10 January 2019, and redacted on 22 January 2019; Decision (ICC-02/04-01/15-1412-Red), 16 January 2019. The 3rd request (ICC-02/04-01/15-1595-Red) was filed on 16 September 2019, and redacted on 3 October 2019; Decision (ICC-02/04-01/15-1622), 1 October 2019. *See* DAJ, paras. 70, 74, 247–255, particularly paras. 251–255; DCB, paras. 79, 120–146.

Note: The Trial Chamber's Rule 135 decisions, cited above, contain procedural history and summaries of the positions of the Defence, Prosecution, Common Legal Representatives of Victims (CLRV) and Legal Representatives for Victims (LRV), with links to the underlying pleadings.

Decision."[36] Thus, the Court forced Mr. Ongwen to forfeit this sacrosanct fair trial right.

The request for a medical examination under Rule 135 may not be usually viewed as a reasonable accommodation. But in this situation, the examination was a request for the Trial Chamber to reasonably accommodate Mr. Ongwen's mental disability so that he could exercise a fundamental fair trial right. Whether a mentally disabled defendant can even make this decision about testifying (or not), and comprehend the potential ramifications of the decision, in the first instance, requires an expert medical examination. Neither the defence lawyer, nor a judge, is equipped to make this medical assessment. This example illustrates that the denial of reasonable accommodation to a mentally disabled defendant resulted in a denial of a fair trial right.

The Court's reasoning in its 1 October 2019 Decision[37] is instructive as to the functioning of its mental disability blindspot. It recognizes that the right to testify is a procedural right of a defendant, which includes an informed decision about whether he wants to exercise this right.[38] In particular, concluding there is no new information about Mr. Ongwen's situation, the Decision refers to previous reports supporting Mr. Ongwen's fitness to stand trial (from 2016 and earlier in 2019) to conclude that there is no indication that a medical examination is necessary. It simply omits the fact that Mr. Ongwen is a mentally disabled defendant whose mental status is not a static phenomenon.

The Trial Chamber failed to provide equal access to justice for Mr. Ongwen at this important fair trial crossroad in the case—where the right to reasonable accommodation intersected with the fair trial right to present a defence. The Chamber's mental disability blindspot prevented it from implementing the principle of equality which applies to all persons before it, including mentally disabled defendants, like Mr. Ongwen.

---

[36] Decision on Defence Request for Leave to Appeal the Decision on Defence Request for Medical Examination of Mr. Ongwen, 15 October 2019, Doc 1640, para. 11. The Trial Chamber denied all the Defence requests for leave to appeal each of the three Rule 135 requests.

[37] Decision on Further Defence Request for a Medical Examination, *Ongwen* (ICC-02/04-01/15-1622), Trial Chamber, 1 October 2019.

[38] *Ibid.*, para. 14.

Part 3: Why a Presumption of Mental Disability for Defendants Is Needed at the ICC

To ensure equality, a presumption of mental disability should be made available to ICC defendants (who can choose to accept or reject it) in the cases the Court adjudicates.

A presumption is a proposition which is assumed credible and therefore true, and applicable to the situation at hand. Those who disagree have the option to disprove or rebut the presumption—arguing its lack of credibility or its falseness; or if they accept it as true, its lack of applicability to the situation. But what is important is that the presumption is a starting point.

The presumption proposed is based on the recognized mass trauma of conflict situations, which comprise the ICC's docket, and the indiscriminate effects of this trauma on people in the conflict area. This means reasonable accommodation for everyone, equally, who is adversely affected by the conflict in the proceedings—regardless of the ICC labels of victims and defendants, who are the alleged perpetrators.[39]

The ICC Is a Ground Zero for War and Conflict

These conflict "situations" are the raison d'être of the ICC for its existence. Case names start with the conflict "situation," that is, "Situation in Uganda in the Case of The Prosecutor v. Dominic Ongwen." The "situation" may be a pre-conflict situation, a continuing and ongoing conflict situation, or a post-conflict situation—or some combination of all of

[39] The trauma experienced by those alleged to be perpetrators is recognized in the notion of perpetrator trauma. *See* Saira Mohamed, *Of Monsters and Men: Perpetrator Trauma and Mass Atrocity*, 115 COLUM. L. REV. 5 (2015) 1157–1216 at 1162 ("...perpetrators can experience their crime as trauma...that is, the commission of the crime itself causes a psychological injury to the perpetrator, which can result in particular adverse physical, social or emotional consequence").

See also Diagnostic Criteria for PTSD, Criterion A.1. which is "directly experiencing the traumatic event[s]" in American Psychiatric Association, THE DIAGNOSTIC AND STATISTICAL MANUAL OF MENTAL DISORDERS ("DSM 5") (5th ed., Washington, D.C/London, APA Publishing, 2013) at 271 and includes "exposure to war as a combatant or civilian" at 254 ("directly experiencing" encompasses both the person who is committing the traumatic act and the person against whom the act is committed).

these. Whatever its status, it is reasonable to assume that war and conflict have inflicted devastating, traumatic and long-lasting effects on everyone within their reach. Mass trauma does not discriminate. It is true that each individual may process the traumas differently: not everyone in a conflict situation has mental health problems, nor do people suffering from mental illness only come from conflict areas. However, differentials in impact do not mitigate its mass nature. There is a general correlation between war and conflict and adverse mental health consequences.[40]

Mass trauma, and the resultant mental health consequences are not limited to the immediate time period of the initial trauma, and can continue—as in the case of child soldiers—over long periods of time and, according to some experts, indefinitely.[41] The form of the trauma may be manifest in mental illness, or in a lesser form of mental distress, or mental disability.[42] Nevertheless, the concept of mental disability—that the person is unable to function in some sphere of her/his daily life, for some periods of time, due to the trauma experienced—is a low threshold.

The Intersection of Mass Trauma and the ICC as an African Court

Since all the cases prosecuted to date (as of May 2024) at the ICC have involved "situations" in Africa and defendants of color from the African

[40] R. Srinivasa Murthy and Rashmi Lakshminarayana, *Mental health consequences of war: a brief review of research findings*, WORLD PSYCHIATRY. 2006 Feb; 5(1): 25–30 (last visited 28 September 2023).

[41] *See* testimony of Defence Child Soldier Expert, Major (ret) Pollar Awich at *Ongwen*, T-203, pp. 65–66.

[42] The American with Disabilities Act (ADA) defines a person with a disability as a person who has a physical or mental impairment that substantially limits one or more major life activity. What is the definition of disability under the ADA? | ADA National Network (adata.org).

The DSM-5 defines mental disorder as a "syndrome characterized by clinically significant disturbance in an individual's cognition, emotion regulation or behavior that reflects a dysfunction in the psychological, biological or developmental processes underlying mental functioning. Mental disorders are usually associated with significant distress or disability in social, occupational, or other important activities...." Use of the Manual at 20.

The terms "mental illness" and "mental disability" are distinct terms and not synonymous. I am proposing that the standard for reasonable accommodation for mental disability is not a criminal standard, as would be applied to a mental disease or defect affirmative defence under Article 31(1)(a).

Continent,[43] the specific studies on the trauma of war and conflict there are particularly relevant. This focus does not reflect a conclusion that trauma is limited to the African continent, or that people who live on the Continent are "more prone" to be traumatized and develop mental illness than those living in war and conflict zones outside of Africa. But the crimes, resulting from centuries of colonialism and imperialism in Africa, provide an essential context and their impact cannot be deleted. Seggane Musisi and Eugene Kinyanda[44] conclude that "trauma, especially war-related mass trauma, is endemic and enigmatic in Africa stretching over 600 years."[45] They cite research over the past two or so decades which documents the "horrendous trauma and stressor-related mental health sequels, following the never-ending enigmatic war-trauma on the African continent."[46] This scholarship should give strong traction to make available a presumption which affects all parties in the cases which the ICC adjudicates.

Thus, based on the subject matter of its cases, and the resulting mass trauma of war and conflict, it would seem that a consciousness about mental disability and the need to provide reasonable accommodations

[43] There are ongoing investigations in Bangladesh/Myanmar, State of Palestine, Republic of the Philippines, Ukraine and Venezuela, but no prosecutions at this time.

[44] Seggane Musisi and Eugene Kinyanda, *Long-term Impact of War, Civil War, and Persecution in Civilian Populations—Conflict and Post-Traumatic Stress in African Communities*, FRONT. PSYCHIATRY, 2020, 11:20; published online 25 February 2020.

See also James Okello, T.S. Onen and Seggane Musisi, *Psychiatric disorders among war-abducted and non-abducted adolescents in Gulu district, Uganda: a comparative study*, AFR. J. PSYCHIATRY (Johannesburg), Vol. 4, November 2007, pp. 225–231 (concludes that "war-abducted children are significantly more affected psychologically and therefore should be screened and assessed for psychiatric problems" and the "majority of children and adolescents in war affected areas have multiple and clinically significant emotional responses to different kinds of traumatic exposure with a high incidence of major depression; generalized anxiety disorder; PTSD; and co-morbidity").

The location of the study was the Gulu district in northern Uganda, the same area where Mr. Ongwen lived when he was abducted by the LRA. The researchers note that the Gulu district had "the longest and most severe experience of the 18-year-old LRA insurgency" and has the largest number of internally displaced persons (IDP) camps, where about 436,239 persons are living. The overwhelming majority of persons in the study were, like Mr. Ongwen, Acholi (91.5% of the abducted group; 95.8% of the non-abducted group). The most significant traumatic experiences were predominantly direct, that is, forced to kill, being forced to perform rituals, being forced to torture and forced to leave home and property.

[45] *Ibid.*, p. 2 (Section on Mass Traumatization in Africa: War and Persecution)

[46] *Ibid.*, p. 3 (Section on Mass Traumatization in Africa: War and Persecution)

should be a "no-brainer." *But this is not the case*. Courts reflect the societies in which they operate, including where there is a low level of awareness about mental disability and mental health. This contributes to a mental disability blindspot, which—on its face—appears incongruous in an international court like the ICC, committed in theory to equality. It is this disconnect, between theory and practice (as evidenced in the *Ongwen* case) for which a presumption of mental disability for defendants, if they choose to invoke it, could bridge the divide.

Mental Disability Should Be Reasonably Accommodated, Based on a Minimal, *Prima Facie* Showing

A presumption of mental disability resulting from the existence of mass trauma is different than grounds for the exclusion of criminal responsibility, under Article 31(1)(a). A mental disability presumption and the ground for excluding criminal responsibility due to mental disease or defect do not share the same legal standards. The legal standard for a presumption of mental disability would be based on a minimal *prima facie* showing, because its object is equal access to justice through reasonable accommodation. This is not a determination or finding on guilt, which is based on the proof beyond a reasonable doubt legal standard.

The evidence of mass trauma should be sufficient as a *prima facie* basis to provide reasonable accommodation for a mentally disabled defendant. A *prima facie* showing for a mentally disabled defendant is simple and direct. Its context is the "situation" of conflict of the case. For an ICC defendant, we are dealing with the easily identifiable markers which are recorded in the Detention Center's records: reports from treating psychologists and psychiatrists, and a treatment regimen for diagnosed mental disorders. There is also the record of requests from the "first responders," the defence counsel, for reasonable accommodation by the Court.

Once a Trial Chamber is informed that a defendant is being treated for mental illness, including with medication, it should accept this as a *prima facie* showing to support reasonable accommodation for mental disability. Whether this mental illness is the basis for excluding criminal responsibility is an independent and different question and the ultimate decision which the Chamber has to make by applying a proof beyond a reasonable doubt standard.

Part 4: Why the Court Got Disability and Reasonable Accommodation Wrong in *Ongwen*—The Mental Disability Blindspot at Work

The onus on defence counsel to identify her/his client's disability to the Court does not absolve the ICC from its legal obligation to reasonably accommodate the disability. So why is it so hard for the ICC to comply with international law and its own Statute in respect to accommodation for all disabled defendants? The short answer is: the Court has a "mental disability blindspot." This was operating in the case of Mr. Ongwen.

The notion of "blindspot," as discussed in Chap. 1,[47] is that one cannot see or is prevented from seeing something: it may be a blindspot while driving which prevents the driver from seeing an oncoming vehicle at an intersection; it may mean that someone simply omits a category or factor in her/his thinking or analysis. The point is that a blindspot obstructs full vision—both physically and mentally. This is detrimental not only to an outcome or result, but also to the person with the blindspot. As *Ongwen* illustrates, the blindspot becomes an obstacle for dispensing equal access to justice, and equal justice for, a disabled defendant, in violation of international law.

When examining how this blindspot operates, it is important to remove the element of intent from the equation. I am not saying that the ICC intends, or individual judges intend, to discriminate against mentally disabled defendants. Nor would such a generalization be supported in all cases. I am saying that that the blindspot makes the Court's

[47] Chapter 1, section on The Operation of Judicial Biases and Blindspots, *supra*.

implementation of full equality difficult, if not impossible, for mentally disabled defendants.

There are a number of observations I have made about the Trial Chamber in the *Ongwen* case, which demonstrate its mental disability blindspot at work:

Observation #1

Based on the Trial Chamber's access to information about Mr. Ongwen's mental health illnesses and treatments, the Trial Chamber *should have known* that Mr. Ongwen, at the time of the trial, was at least mentally disabled and, in the expert opinion of some professionals, suffering from mental illnesses. Mr. Ongwen's mental disability required reasonable accommodation in order for him to fully access and meaningfully participate in the judicial process of his trial.

All of the "identifiable markers" (reports, lists of medications, etc.) were available to the *Ongwen* Trial Chamber. The Chamber had access to the initial reports of the Defence Experts and Court-Appointed Expert, who had examined Mr. Ongwen in late 2016 and early 2017,[48] as well as regular reports from Detention Center psychologists, psychiatrists and other personnel who closely monitored Mr. Ongwen and his treatment (including medication) regimens.

The Defence efforts to put the Trial Chamber on notice of Mr. Ongwen's mental illnesses and disabilities, their impact on his fair trial rights and the need to reasonably accommodate him (through scheduling and other logistics) and the multiple requests for Rule 135 medical examinations spanned over years and are detailed in the Defence pleadings.[49]

---

[48] The Court ordered a psychiatric examination by Professor Joop T. de Jong on 16 December 2016 (ten days *after* the beginning of the trial) to assess Mr. Ongwen's mental state at the time of the examination and provide recommendations to the Detention Centre to address any mental conditions or disorders he found. *See*, TJ: 2576–2578. *This was not an order to determine if Mr. Ongwen was competent to stand trial.* The Court had already determined, on its own, that he was fit for trial because it accepted his plea of not guilty on 6 December, when the trial started with the Prosecution's Opening Statement.

[49] *See* DCB, paras. 120–146, 529–674; TJ: 106–115, 2448–2580; DAJ, paras. 69–76, 247–255, 320–419; DAS, paras. 49–50, 151–188; AJ, paras. 422–450, 1105–1384.

Moreover, the documentation of Mr. Ongwen's mental status from numerous sources reflects that he had a history of mental illness and treatment, which started decades before the opening of trial in early December 2016 and is ongoing. The Defence Experts concluded that Mr. Ongwen's mental illnesses stemmed from his forced abduction by the LRA around 1987, continued through his years in the LRA and still plague him today.[50]

Throughout the trial, the Trial Chamber made a few logistical accommodations (albeit late), for example, in the scheduling of trial sessions, in response to both the Detention Centre recommendations and at the initiative and repeated insistence of the Defence.[51] The Chamber, however, never acted affirmatively, on its own initiative, to reasonably accommodate Mr. Ongwen's disability. The Chamber never asked Mr. Ongwen, for example, what it could do to make the trial process more accessible to him, given his history of mental illness and treatment and the reports from the ICC professionals at the Detention Centre.

The obvious question is: Did the Trial Chamber ignore the "markers" or misread the reports? If it didn't, then how did it process the information about Mr. Ongwen's mental state? Why did the Trial Chamber fail to reasonably accommodate Mr. Ongwen in the proceedings to ensure his fair trial rights?

I do not think that the Trial Chamber saw Mr. Ongwen as mentally disabled.

From the very beginning of the trial, the Trial Chamber did not consider Mr. Ongwen as a mentally disabled defendant. First, in early December 2016, right before the opening of the trial, Mr. Ongwen was asked to enter a plea to the charges in the Confirmation of Charges document. Before this hearing, the Defence made a motion for a Rule 135 medical (psychiatric) examination of Mr. Ongwen, to determine if he was fit for trial, and requested a postponement of the "plea proceeding" until this examination was completed. The Defence informed the Judges

---

[50] *See* DCB, para. 537, n.889 which refers to Defence Experts' Second Report, UGA-D26-0015-0948, pp. 23–27 (noting, for example, chronic exposure to life-threatening traumatic experiences from 1986; hospitalization in Juba for mental illness after battle in 1997, incidents of loss of consciousness reported in 1996, 1997, 1999 and 2002).

[51] DCB, para. 145 (initial Detention Centre recommendations re scheduling not implemented by Trial Chamber until eight months later).

that it had received a preliminary report from its own expert psychiatrists which concluded that Mr. Ongwen did not understand the charges brought against him at the ICC. The Chamber rejected the motion, and proceeded with "business as usual," notwithstanding that Mr. Ongwen's mental health status could impact on his ability to comprehend the charges against him.

In fact, toward the end of the trial, in rejecting yet again one of the Defence requests for a medical (psychiatric) examination of Mr. Ongwen, the Trial Chamber indicated that it "never considered" whether Mr. Ongwen was mentally disabled.[52] The Chamber's repeated rejections of requests for a medical (psychiatric) examination lead to the conclusion that the issues of mental health were not factors in its analysis of Mr. Ongwen. Mr. Ongwen's mental disability did not appear to be on the Chamber's radar. The Chamber was always laser focused on the ultimate question (criminal responsibility) when it evaluated any mental health information about Mr. Ongwen, including requests for reasonable accommodation of his disability. It could not and did not accept, at a minimum, that Mr. Ongwen was mentally disabled. Its blindspot caused the Trial Chamber to miss "markers" or "red flags" for mental disability and mental illness.

Observation #2

Following from its inability to "see" and reasonably accommodate mental disability, the ICC Judges[53] failed to apply common sense and knowledge in reaching their conclusions on mental illness and mental disability. One does not have to be a trained psychologist or psychiatrist to realize that Mr. Ongwen would have been suffering adverse mental health

[52] Decision on Defence Request for Leave to Appeal the Decision on Defence Request for Medical Examination of Mr. Ongwen, *Ongwen* (ICC-02/04-01/15-1640), Trial Chamber, 16 October 2019, para. 11. In the Chamber's Decision rejecting the leave request, para. 11, it stated: "The question of whether the accused may be mentally disabled was never considered in the Impugned Decision. Bearing this in mind, the question of whether the Chamber discriminated against the accused 'as a mentally disabled defendant' also does not arise from the Impugned Decision."

[53] I am referring to "ICC Judges" collectively at both the trial and appellate levels, given that the Appeals Chamber affirmed and bolstered the Trial Judgment.

consequences, based simply on his situation: he was a victim of the LRA, abducted from his family as a child of 8 or 9, indoctrinated by the LRA, forced to commit heinous acts and subjected to the horrific, sadistic and criminal rules of Joseph Kony, and repeatedly punished in the LRA for his unsuccessful efforts to try to escape.

Yet, in its Judgment, the Trial Chamber concludes that Mr. Ongwen's abduction is irrelevant to the charges,[54] and carves out an "Ongwen Exception"[55] to the toxic, and often lethal, traumatic effects of the LRA on Kony's abductees. The Judgment recounts evidence of initiation rituals, standing rules, indoctrination and Kony's brutal disciplinary regime,[56] but it is silent on how these rituals and practices affected the conduct and mental state of Mr. Ongwen. The Trial Chamber is implicitly saying that Mr. Ongwen was unaffected by the brutality and bestiality in the LRA.

Mr. Ongwen graphically described his first failed attempt to escape, shortly after he was abducted in 1987, at the Sentence Hearing:

> The first thing you are told is do not escape. If you escape, the end result is death .... They asked us – they started by asking me, "Kadogo, why did you escape?" I told them I was going to see my mother and father. Then they told us that, "Your mother and father are no more. They were killed." I thought that they were actually deceiving me, but that was the truth .... And they [abductees who had tried to escape but were brought back to the LRA] were tied up, they were hung on a tree. Then they gave us a very sharp knife. The two of us each were given a knife and we were ordered to kill these people. I told them I had never killed in my life and I had never seen a dead person. They told us, "If you want to live, kill these people." ... I was beaten with a wire lock. They ordered us to slaughter these people with a knife, remove their intestines and hang their intestines on the tree. Part of their intestines we were ordered to hang on our necks, and we were told to say this was an electric wire. We did all that .... We sat where blood was dripping, and they put our plate of beans under the people who were dripping, the bodies that were dripping with blood and the blood was dripping on those plates .... So we were forced to eat beans mixed with human

---

[54] TJ: 27, 2592.

[55] *See* DAJ: 5, 441, 380.

[56] TJ: 906–930.

> blood. Even though I grew up in the bush, I know that in Acholi culture humans are not eaten. I don't know if there are other tribes or clans that eat people, but in Acholi human beings cannot be eaten .... Every time I saw meat, I would vomit. Up to now, I do not like to eat meat ... I will go to my grave with that image in my mind. Whatever happens, I cannot forget that image. It is imprinted in my image now.[57]

He describes another failed escape plan in 2002.[58] In total, Mr. Ongwen made five failed attempts to escape.

Was the Trial Chamber "clueless" about the plight of child soldiers? Of course not. But factors were operating which made it impossible for it to accept Mr. Ongwen as a child soldier victim, and a victim of the LRA's trafficking of child abductees. One of the pivotal factors was the Chamber's mental disability blindspot, which prevented it from "seeing" the continuing adverse mental health consequences of child soldiering on Mr. Ongwen, even after he reached the age of 18.[59]

Observation #3: The Trial Chamber Conflated Mental Illness and Mental Disability

Courts adjudicate a defendant's mental status in many situations: Judges decide the fitness of a defendant to stand trial and meaningfully participate in her/his defence; whether an affirmative defence based on mental disease or defect is a basis to exclude criminal responsibility; and whether a defendant's mental illness is a mitigating factor at sentence. Each circumstance requires different standards, which may vary from Court to Court. But at the ICC (and at other criminal courts), the highest standard—proof beyond a reasonable doubt—is reserved for the

[57] Transcript, Sentence Hearing, *Ongwen* (ICC-02/04-01/15-T-261-ENG ET WT), 15 April 2021 at T-261, p. 5, ll. 6–25, p. 6, ll. 1–25 and p. 7, ll. 1–18.

[58] Transcript, Sentence Hearing, T-261, p. 15, ll. 1–25 to p. 16, ll. 1–13; *see also* p. 10, ll. 18–25 to p. 11, ll. 1–22. *See* DCB, para. 440, n.508 (Prof. de Jong's report documents five failed escape attempts made by Mr. Ongwen while in the LRA; *see also*, references to escape attempts in Defence Experts' First Report).

[59] *See* Charles A. Taku and Beth S. Lyons, *The Ongwen Judgments: A Stain on International Justice*, J. INT. CRIM. JUSTICE, 2024, mqae044, https://doi.org/10.1093/jicj/mqae044

determination of guilt. At the ICC, the lesser standard of balance of probabilities applies to mitigating circumstances for sentence.[60]

The concepts of mental illness as a defence, and the need to reasonably accommodate a mental disability are distinct legal concepts, based on different legal standards. This distinction must be made, for the purposes of equality in the proceedings, between a defendant's mental illness and her/his mental disability. Mental illness and mental disability are not fungible.

But, the problem is that the two concepts, which admittedly are intertwined to some degree, often get tangled at the expense of the defendant with the mental disability. This is what happened in the *Ongwen* case. The Trial Chamber commingled these two notions: it seemed to think that providing reasonable accommodations to a mentally disabled Mr. Ongwen could be construed as support for the Defence case that he suffered from a number of mental illnesses which excluded criminal responsibility. The Judges' mental disability blindspot made it impossible for them to untangle the concepts, and distinguish between disability and illness.

Observation #4: "Visible Normalcy" Is Misleading and Not a Reliable or Relevant Criterion for Either Mental Disability or Mental Illness

The Trial Chamber erroneously relied on its own assessment that Mr. Ongwen "looked normal" to conclude that Mr. Ongwen was neither mentally disabled nor suffering from mental diseases. The Judges had access to psychiatric reports, including from the Defence Experts, the Court-Appointed Expert and the Detention Centre, which supported—at a minimum—that Mr. Ongwen was plagued with, and being treated for, mental health issues. Yet, the Judges gave almost exclusive weight to their own observations in Court of Mr. Ongwen's mental state: he appeared "normal" and appeared to interact "normally" with team

[60] *Ongwen* Judgment on Sentence, 6 May 2021, para. 54

members and guards in the courtroom. Hence, the Chamber concluded that he was not mentally disabled or mentally ill.

The Trial Chamber substituted its own observations of Mr. Ongwen in Court for the opinion of the Defence Experts, who had examined him on multiple occasions and produced reports for the Court over a three-year period. In these reports, the Defence Experts concluded that Mr. Ongwen was suffering from numerous mental illnesses. Watching Mr. Ongwen in Court, day after day for years, left the Chamber with a wrong impression of his mental status.

First, the Judges were observing a mentally ill Mr. Ongwen who was taking medications, which made it possible for the trial schedule to proceed virtually uninterrupted. He "looked normal," and was polite and non-disruptive in court.

In fact, during the almost four years of trial, Mr. Ongwen rarely reacted visibly to Prosecution witnesses as they testified. Three exceptions come to mind during the Prosecution's case: one involved a Prosecution witness who testified about the UPDF's killing of Mr. Ongwen's brother; a second occurred during the testimony of Prosecution Expert Dr. Mezey, whom Mr. Ongwen saw as Joseph Kony; and a third was during testimony about the killing of his parents. Considering that there were 231 court hearings, which included 69 Prosecution witnesses, 54 Defence witnesses, 7 Victims' witnesses,[61] these three examples are infinitesimal, however painful and traumatic they were to Mr. Ongwen.

Throughout the trial, Ongwen was still suffering from mental illnesses. The Defence Experts Professor Ovuga and Dr. Akena diagnosed severe depressive illness, post-traumatic stress disorder (PTSD), dissociative disorder (including depersonalization and multiple identity disorder), severe suicidal ideation and a high risk of committing suicide, as well as dissociative amnesia and symptoms of obsessive compulsive disorder.[62] The Court-Appointed Expert, Professor Joop de Jong, concurred with the three fundamental diagnoses (major depressive disorder

[61] ICC Press Release, "ICC Trial Chamber IX to deliberate on the *Ongwen* case," 12 March 2020.

[62] *See* DCB, paras, 536–7.

[MDD], PTSD and other specified dissociative disorder) and characterized the MDD and PTSD as severe.[63]

Mental illness does not display its symptoms 24/7, so Mr. Ongwen could have appeared "normal" at times to the Judges, while he was still suffering from mental illnesses. If an illness is not manifesting physically, it would be undetectable to the Judges, or any other person observing Mr. Ongwen at the trial. But, the problem is that the Trial Chamber substituted its lay observations for the diagnoses of three medical experts, based on their clinical examinations of Mr. Ongwen. Hence, it is wrong to conclude (as the Trial Chamber did), based on visual assessments during trial, that Mr. Ongwen was processing the trial as a mentally able person, free from mental illness.

When Mr. Ongwen was suffering from dissociative disorders while in Court and unable to focus or concentrate and "spaced out," this was not apparent just by looking at him. Mr. Ongwen admitted to the Trial Chamber at the Sentence Hearing, and to the Appeals Chamber during appellate arguments, that he only understood about 40% in the proceedings, and did not understand 60% of what was said.[64]

Some may argue that a Judge's observations of a mentally ill and mentally disabled defendant can be compared to judging any witness's demeanor. This is not true. Even a Judge who is experienced in deciding cases involving mental health issues is not a medical expert who can make an accurate medical diagnosis by observation. In addition, the Judges, no doubt, were well aware of the medication regimen, which had to affect Mr. Ongwen's conduct and may explain why there were so few outbursts in Court.

This illustrates the importance of "mental health literacy" for Judges,[65] as well as defence counsel and others who interact with a defendant with mental health problems. But, mental health literacy improves only when one is open to "seeing" mental health issues. This is where the blindspot obstruction applies: if you are <u>not</u> looking for something, there is a high likelihood you will miss it—as the Trial Chamber missed the markers, or "red flags" of mental disability in the *Ongwen* case.

---

[63] *Ibid.*, para. 540.

[64] Transcript, *Ongwen* Sentence Hearing, p. 4, ll. 8–14; Transcript, Appeals Hearing, *Ongwen* (ICC-02/04-01/15-T-267-ENG ET WT), T-267, 18 February 2022, p. 35, ll. 5–7.

[65] *See*, Chapter 1, n.262, n. 263.

Part 5: What Is to Be Done?

Key Proposals: A Presumption and Self-evaluation

For the ICC to affirmatively comply with international law and the Rome Statute in respect to reasonable accommodation for all disabled defendants:

1. The ICC should make a presumption of mental disability available to all those persons involved in the ICC's war and conflict "situations," both the Court-accepted victims and the defendants on trial, who are the alleged perpetrators. As previously discussed, it is a defendant's choice whether or not to avail her/himself of this presumption.
2. The ICC needs to examine and remedy the Court's practices—in the courtroom and in its structure—in respect to reasonable accommodation for disability, including mental disability. This means acknowledging that a disability blindspot exists and exploring how it operates at the ICC, including at the judicial decision-making level.

Implementation

To effectively implement the above:

1. **The mental health literacy of everyone involved in a case needs to be "upped."** This applies to Judges, to all Parties, to all court personnel. Mental illness is complex, and within the court system, each of us, regardless of our position, would benefit from knowing more and being able to accurately observe and identify problems in a quicker, more comprehensive fashion. The goal is not to transform persons into psychologists or psychiatrists; but to enable those who interact with the defendant to be better informed observers, who can identify when assistance and reasonable accommodation is needed.
2. **The welfare of the mentally disabled defendant should be the paramount, common principle which dictates the working relations between the Court, Detention Center experts and Defence experts.**

It is not always easy for experts inside the court detention system to share and exchange information with the Defence experts: the bureaucracy is often formidable and designed to discourage any sharing. The purpose of sharing is not to transform Defence Experts into the medical personnel of the Detention Centre, who are providing the day-to-day treatment to the defendant, but to add more expertise to benefit the defendant. A defendant may have stronger and different levels of trust and expectation in experts who are working for the Defence, than in those appointed by the judicial and detention systems. For example, cultural or language issues may exist which can have an enormous impact on communication between the defendant and the treating professionals in the detention center. Specific proposals need to be made on a case-by-case basis, but it is hard to imagine that *not* sharing information would benefit the well-being of a mentally disabled defendant.

3. **Medication regimens need to be shared with the Defence teams, as a matter of right to information of the defendant**. A defendant may be medicated both to address a medical condition, as well as to enable her or him to be present at the trial. The Judges may be concerned with how to avert mental health crises in the courtroom, which impact on the efficiency and continuity of the trial. Defence counsel need to know that the defendant is, in fact, able to concentrate on the evidence presented, in order to assist in her/his own defence. Knowledge of medications and possible side effects is essential information which a Defence team needs from professionals who are treating the defendant in the Detention Centre.

Suggestions for Structural Proposals, Which Would Signal Institutional Awareness and a Commitment to Equality for Disabled Persons at the ICC

1. **Anti-discrimination unit at the ICC**. Just as the ICC has instituted structural responses to gender (in)equality, for example, by establishing its Focal Point/Office on Gender Equality, a similar effort has to

be made for people with disabilities. Essentially, this is a compliance unit (like those found in corporations and businesses) which would monitor and ensure compliance in the ICC's practices and policies with international law for disabled persons.

2. **Equality forum**. The ICC has to ask the disabled: what can we do for you, to improve access to justice. Another name for this, used by election and advertising campaigns, etc. is focus group. This needs to be a permanent forum which regularly convenes meetings and reports back to the ICC; the ICC, in turn, would report back to the Forum on its progress in implementing equality in respect to access to justice for the disabled.
3. **Budget should be allocated to the ICC's Counsel Support Section (CSS), so it can provide financial and other resources to address the reasonable accommodations for physically and mentally disabled defendants, represented by the Defence teams.**
4. **The right of the defendant to family life is an important support for all defendants, and especially for mentally disabled defendants**. The right to family life applies to all who are incarcerated. The violation of this right is detrimental to everyone. But the importance of family contact, and the sufferings when it is withheld and does not occur, may affect a mentally disabled defendant differently, because of disability and result in more serious consequences.
5. **The Rome Statute should be amended to include disability.** Article 21(3), which currently relegates disability to the catch-all of "other status," should be amended to include disability as a prohibited basis for discrimination. Similarly, crimes against persons with disabilities should be enumerated in Articles 7 (crimes against humanity) and 8 (war crimes).[66]

[66] *See* n.13 *supra*.

Conclusion

The battle for reasonable accommodation for Mr. Ongwen's mental disability demonstrates a fundamental truism: any right guaranteed under law is hollow if it cannot be implemented. Whether the ICC can make good on its mandate for equal access to justice for defendants who are disabled depends on whether it can look at its policies, practices and jurisprudence through a prism of equality, unobstructed by any blindspot.

3

Conclusions

Abstract This concluding chapter presents the fundamental question throughout the book: is it "just" bias and blindspots, or is it legal racism and culturalism? The ICC's double standards for justice and accountability, its Western (only) cultural presumptions and its lens of whiteness have produced a track record of selective investigation and prosecution. These factors have been the backbone of judicial unfairness, which corrodes and erodes the legitimacy of international justice. The racism and culturalism reflected in the jurisprudence of the *Ongwen* Judgment underscore the urgent imperative of the struggles for equality and fairness on which the legitimacy of international justice hinges.

Keywords Race • Racism • Culture • Culturalism • Whiteness • White supremacy • Western cultural assumptions • Double standards • Selective prosecution • Palestine • Afghanistan • Ukraine

Race and culture shape everyone, and everything, everywhere, including at the International Criminal Court (ICC). As Leigh Swigart has commented, "culture shapes the perceptions and practices of *everyone* involved

B. S. Lyons, *Race, Culture and Mental Illness in the International Criminal Court's Ongwen Judgment: Biases and Blindspots*, https://doi.org/10.1007/978-3-031-73683-4_3

in the international justice project."[1] The "ubiquity of culture" means that culture permeates everything, including law, which is often presented as "neutral, objective and independent of cultural concerns."[2] To this observation, I would add that law is also presented as race-neutral, despite the plethora of evidence to the contrary, and that race and culture are often intertwined. Tim Kelsall has produced a detailed study of judicial approaches to culture at the Special Court for Sierra Leone (SCSL) and the problems of trying cases in a Western-style international court, which involve cultures not within this Western sphere. He has concluded that "[c]ulture matters, and for justice to be done, the international community must adapt to this fact."[3]

No doubt, one could generate a range of structural and organizational proposals which would provide a framework for the ICC to potentially remedy the biases and blindspots discussed in this book, and which would compensate all the victims for the judicial deficits in the areas of race and culture. Chapters 1 and 2 have suggested some possible remedies, including (1) a review (and potential revision) of past ICC decisions through the prism of race and culture; (2) amendment of sentencing rules to include culture, race and disability as factors to be considered as individual circumstances in sentencing; (3) inclusion of traditional justice mechanisms in sentencing under the rubric of complementarity; (4) availability of a presumption of mental disability to defendants from conflict situations which they can choose to invoke (or not); (5) organizational structures and procedures which would provide equal access to justice for mentally disabled defendants; (6) amendments to the Rome Statute, Articles 7 (crimes against humanity) and 8 (war crimes) to

---

[1] INTERSECTIONS, Leigh Swigart, Chapter 2, p. 36 (discussing the fundamental link between language and culture at the ICC) (italics in original).

[2] Julie Fraser and Brianne McGonigle Leyh, Editors, INTERSECTIONS, Introduction, p. 4.

[3] *See* Tim Kelsall, CULTURE UNDER CROSS-EXAMINATION, INTERNATIONAL JUSTICE AND THE SPECIAL COURT FOR SIERRA LEONE (Cambridge University Press, 2009) p. 267. Based on this study of cultural issues and context at the SCSL in the CDF, RUF, AFRC and Charles Taylor trials, Kelsall concludes that the Court was either oblivious to, or paid little or no attention to, local cultural realities in Sierra Leone, and that this impacted on its jurisprudence. Chapter 3 discusses judicial insensitivity to cultural factors in determining command responsibility in the CDF case. Chapter 5 focuses on the importance of cultural considerations in understanding child soldiering, and prosecuting the crime of enlisting soldiers under the age of 15.

include crimes against disabled persons, and Article 21(3) to include disability as a category of discrimination.

But no proposal can be successfully implemented without agreement on its purpose, or at least, acknowledgment of the problem(s) it is supposed to remedy. At a minimum, there needs to be some underlying ideological unity that addressing biases and blindspots is necessary for legitimacy and fairness. This would "level the legal playing field" so that international justice—in this case, as expressed at the ICC—can live up to its promise to provide accountability and justice to the people in the "situations" the ICC adjudicates. It should be a "given" then, that for the ICC to confront its racial and cultural biases and blindspots, it must (1) acknowledge that biases and blindspots exist; and (2) analyze how these operate within its structures as well as (3) within the decisions and judgments which it renders.

But none of this is possible while international justice, including at the ICC, continues its pattern and practice of adjudicating cases based on Western (only) presumptions and an exclusive lens of "whiteness" and prosecuting only one side of the "conflict" situation on its docket.

Selective prosecution and double standards have been the norm at the ICC since its inception.[4] The glaring fact is that, in its 22 years of existence, the ICC has prosecuted only defendants of color from the African Continent, thus effectively "criminalizing Blackness," as Rachel López has concluded.[5] As of May 2024, there have been no prosecutions of Western or white defendants. And, until the ICC Chief Prosecutor Khan's 20 May 2024 application for arrests warrants for both Israeli and Hamas leaders in the Situation in the State of Palestine—only one side of the conflict in the ICC "situations" has been investigated and prosecuted.

The *Ongwen* case follows in this pattern: Black defendant and no prosecution of the Ugandan government and its defense forces (UPDF) for

---

[4] John Reynolds and Sujith Xavier, *"The Dark Corners of the World" TWAIL and International Criminal Justice*, J. INT. CRIM. JUSTICE 14(2016), 959–983.

[5] Rachel López, "*Black Guilt, White Guilt at the International Criminal Court*," in Matiangai V. S. Sirleaf (ed.), *RACE AND NATIONAL SECURITY* (New York, 2023; online edn, Oxford Academic, 21 Sept. 2023), https://doi.org/10.1093/oso/9780197754641.003.0012, Chapter 11, p. 211 ("with these convictions [of Black men], the ICC builds on a long history of criminalizing Blackness") (accessed 21 May 2024).

well-documented crimes, including allegations of genocide in Northern Uganda,[6] committed in its war against the LRA.

Whether the ICC can "break this mold" remains to be seen. In March 2023, Pre-Trial Chamber II of the ICC issued arrest warrants for Russian President Vladimir Putin and Presidential Commissioner for Children's Rights Maria Lvova-Belova, for allegations of war crimes for unlawful deportation and the transfer of children in the situation in Ukraine.

On 20 May 2024, in the Situation in the State of Palestine, the ICC Chief Prosecutor applied for arrest warrants for Benjamin Netanyahu, the Prime Minister of Israel and Yoav Gallant, the Minister of Defence as well as for Yahya Sinwar, the head of Hamas in the Gaza Strip, Mohammed Diab Ibrahim Al-Masri, Commander-in-Chief of Hamas' military wing, the Al-Qassam Brigades and Ismail Haniyeh, head of Hamas' Political Bureau based on reasonable grounds that war crimes and crimes against humanity had been committed, from at least 7 October 2023 by Hamas and from at least 8 October 2023 by Israel.[7]

But, the ICC Chief Prosecutor did not include Israel's crimes of genocide and apartheid against the Palestinian people—in Gaza, the West Bank and East Jerusalem—in the Application. This is a fundamental and grievous omission, especially since the International Court of Justice (ICJ), on 26 January 2024, in a near-unanimous ruling, held that South Africa presented a "plausible" case that Israel was violating the Genocide Convention[8] in Gaza and ordered Israel to implement provisional measures to prevent the commission of all genocidal acts.[9] Since that time, the ICJ has issued Orders again on 28 March 2024 and 24 May 2024. The May Order states:

> …The Court considers that, in conformity with its obligations under the Genocide Convention, Israel must immediately halt its military offensive,

---

[6] Olara A. Otunnu, *The Secret Genocide*, FOREIGN POLICY, 19 October 2009. *See*, Chapter 1, n.10, *supra*.

[7] Press Release: Statement of ICC Prosecutor Karim A.A. Khan QC: Applications for arrest warrants in the situation in the State of Palestine, 20 May 2024.

[8] Application instituting proceedings and request for the indication of provisional measures (icj-cij.org)

[9] Order of 26 January 2024 (icj-cij.org)

> and any other action in the Rafah Governorate, which may inflict on the Palestinian group in Gaza conditions of life that could bring about its physical destruction in whole or in part.[10]

To date,[11] despite its claims to the contrary, Israel has not complied with the ICJ Orders and no decision has been rendered by the ICC Pre-Trial Chamber I on the arrest warrants.

Statements by the ICC Chief Prosecutor Khan on the Situation in the Islamic Republic of Afghanistan ("Afghanistan") suggest that the ICC's racist/double standard mold for defendant selection remains intact. In 2022, the Court authorized the re-opening of the investigation in the Situation in Afghanistan.[12] In September 2021, Khan announced that if authorization was granted by the Court to resume investigations into the Situation in Afghanistan, he would focus on crimes allegedly committed by the Taliban and the Islamic State and deprioritize other aspects of the investigation—due to limited resources.[13] These "other aspects" include allegations of war crimes committed by U.S. armed forces and CIA, both in Afghanistan and in CIA "black sites" in other ICC countries with a nexus to Afghanistan, starting in May 2003—as detailed in former Chief Prosecutor Fatou Bensouda's original Request in November 2017 to Pre-Trial Chamber III, pursuant to Article 15, to open a formal investigation.[14] This "deprioritization" provides effective immunity to the U.S. government and the CIA for their war crimes and crimes against humanity. This means that the victims of these crimes will never receive justice and reparations.[15]

---

[10] ICJ Order: Application of the Convention on the Prevention and Punishment of the Crime of Genocide in the Gaza Strip (South Africa v. Israel) - Question of Palestine, para. 50.

[11] As of early June 2024.

[12] ICC judges approve request to reopen Afghanistan probe | AP News.

[13] OTP Press Statement, 27 September 2021.

[14] Prosecutor's Request, 20 November 2017 at CR2017_06891.PDF (icc-cpi.int)

[15] ICC Chief Prosecutor Fatou Bensouda opened a preliminary investigation into the Situation in the Islamic Republic of Afghanistan in 2006. Her 2017 Request, in respect to the U.S., states that "information available provides a reasonable basis to believe that members of the United States of America ("US") armed forces and members of the Central Intelligence Agency ('CIA') committed acts of torture, cruel treatment, outrages upon personal dignity, rape and sexual violence against conflict-related detainees in Afghanistan and other locations, principally in the 2003–2004 period" (para. 4). These allegations are detailed in the Request, at paras. 187–252.

The ICC's selective prosecution and double standards of justice, manifest in its pattern and practice of Western (only) cultural presumptions and its lens of "whiteness," have been the backbone of judicial unfairness. All this matters because the ICC's unfairness corrodes and erodes its legitimacy. Racism and white supremacy—in the legal context—produce and reflect a legal racism and culturism, which intersect with each other.

By "legal racism," I am referring to a judgment's holdings and not to any individual racial *animus* of a particular judge. Racism permeates law, including international criminal law, at many levels—structurally, procedurally and in its jurisprudence.[16] As Kamari Clarke points out, white supremacy and racial injustice provided the framework in which the ICC's Rome Statute was developed, and in which the Court operates.[17]

By "culturalism," I mean the failure of the ICC to consider cultural aspects, both of the "situations" before it and the alleged perpetrators being prosecuted. As a result, the ICC fails to make an analysis of the full context in which the crimes occurred—including the social, economic, religious, psychological, historical and cultural factors—and how this context affected the alleged perpetrator. This includes, for example, the omission of cultural factors in applying the Rome Statute grounds for excluding criminal responsibility under Article 31, in determinations of command responsibility and in sentencing.

---

[16] *See*, Kamari Maxine Clarke, Negotiating Racial Injustice: How International Criminal Law Helps Entrench Structural Inequality (justsecurity.org) (power and role of white supremacy re Rome Statute); Derrick A. Bell, Jr., RACE, RACISM AND AMERICAN LAW, 2nd Edition (Little, Brown and Company: 1990) (how racism is manifest in U.S. laws, statutes, jurisprudence).

[17] Clarke, in her article *supra* at n.16, explains that white supremacy is structured into the ICC's Rome Statute, based on the following: (1) identification of "core crimes," which lists the crime of apartheid under crimes against humanity in Article 7 (1)(j)), but not as an Article 5 "core crime"; (2) the "legality" principle and jurisdiction of the ICC which begins July 2002 and omits jurisdiction over the crimes of colonialism and neocolonialization, and as the sources of other crimes; (3) sovereign inequality in the deferral power of the Security Council; (4) double standards of justice which prosecute crimes of alleged perpetrators from African Continent, while being unable to prosecute U.S. officials for crimes in Afghanistan or Abu Graib in Iraq and in other similar situations; and (5) the effects of white supremacy in Article 17 admissibility assessments as to whether States are "willing or unable" to carry out investigations. She also points out that the Rome Statute does not address root causes of violence, including colonialism and neo-colonialism, economic crimes inflicted on the global South, etc., and the root causes of atrocities, especially when they exist because of the colonial powers.

Is It "Just" Bias and Blindspots, or Is It Legal Racism and Culturalism?

The approach of this book, using *Ongwen* as a case study, has been to identify the judicial racial and cultural biases and blindspots embedded in the Trial Chamber's jurisprudence at trial and sentence, and analyze what went wrong. Readers of earlier drafts, particularly of Chap. 1, made two insightful comments: (1) the term "bias" does not reflect the root of the problem, which is racism, and its depth and severity in the *Ongwen* case; (2) the racial bias/blindspot analysis does not address the heart of the problem—racism and white supremacy. I concur that biases and blindspots are the "tips of the icebergs" of the ICC's racism and culturalism. Standing alone, they cannot convey the endemic nature of the racism and culturalism, as it seeps into all aspects of the Court—from case selection to sentencing.

The ultimate question which the *Ongwen* Judgment[18] presents for international justice is: Is it enough to "just" identify judicial biases and blindspots, or, do these add up to legal racism and culturalism, and at what point? Do biases adequately reflect the political context in which they are bred and operate? Does jurisprudential bias reflect institutional racism and culturalism? Does a bias/blindspot analysis negate or omit the systemic nature of the problem?

These questions are the "elephants in the room."

Neither the *Ongwen* Judgment, nor its biases and blindspots, exist in a political vacuum. The ICC's jurisprudence cannot be excised from the world in which it operates, and courtrooms are not hermetic containers, sealed off from politics outside. The racial and cultural biases in the *Ongwen* Judgment exist within a society whose operating systems—in law, health care, education, politics, economics, etc.—have a default setting of white supremacy and Western cultural norms. The international justice system replicates this.

---

[18] Throughout the book I have focused on the *Ongwen* Trial Judgment, which was affirmed by the Appeal Judgment. Thus, the analysis of jurisprudence in the Trial Judgment is also applicable to the Appeal Judgment.

But the *Ongwen* case challenged the ICC's default settings: for example, by making spiritualism a key component of its duress defence, by presenting evidence of the cultural and racial components of its mental disease or defect defence, and by advocating complementarity with traditional justice mechanisms, particularly in sentencing.

The "bias/blindspot analysis" is only a piece of the picture, but it contributes to the systemic analysis. It is necessary to look at all of the effects and manifestations of racism and culturalism in the legal arena, including in jurisprudence—if there is going to be any change in international justice.

To this end, I return to the *Ongwen* case. Whether the *Ongwen* case is memorialized as the "textbook example" of legal racism and culturalism within international criminal jurisprudence is up to the ICC's *Ongwen* Judges. It boils down to whether the Judges possess the judicial courage to ask the question: If Mr. Ongwen were white, and from a Western/European culture, would the Trial Chamber have reached the same conclusions in its Judgment?

If the answer is "no," then the Judges must rectify the jurisprudential injustices. This is not simply an act of remedying a legal wrong; it is also an opportunity to demonstrate that the ICC has the capacity to become an institution whose legitimacy is founded on fairness, inclusivity and a respect for human rights.

But if the answer to the question continues, as it now stands, to be "yes," then the ICC, and by extension, the international justice project, is digging its own grave of illegitimacy even deeper.

Index[1]

[1] Note: Page numbers followed by 'n' refer to notes.

B. S. Lyons, *Race, Culture and Mental Illness in the International Criminal Court's Ongwen Judgment: Biases and Blindspots*, https://doi.org/10.1007/978-3-031-73683-4

GPSR Compliance
The European Union's (EU) General Product Safety Regulation (GPSR) is a set of rules that requires consumer products to be safe and our obligations to ensure this.

If you have any concerns about our products, you can contact us on

ProductSafety@springernature.com

In case Publisher is established outside the EU, the EU authorized representative is:

Springer Nature Customer Service Center GmbH
Europaplatz 3
69115 Heidelberg, Germany

www.ingramcontent.com/pod-product-compliance
Lightning Source LLC
Chambersburg PA
CBHW071951150525
PP16506900001BA/8
9783031736827